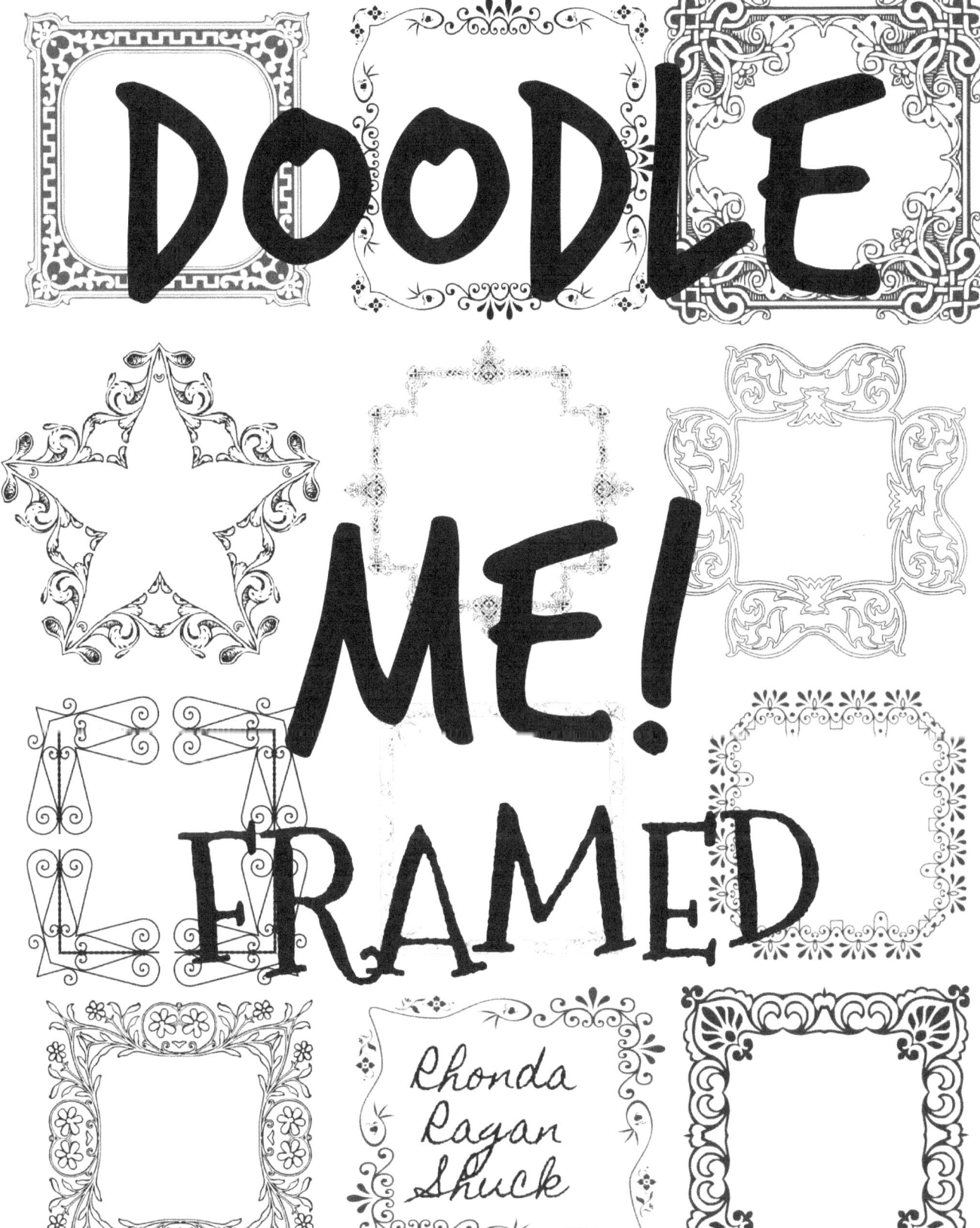

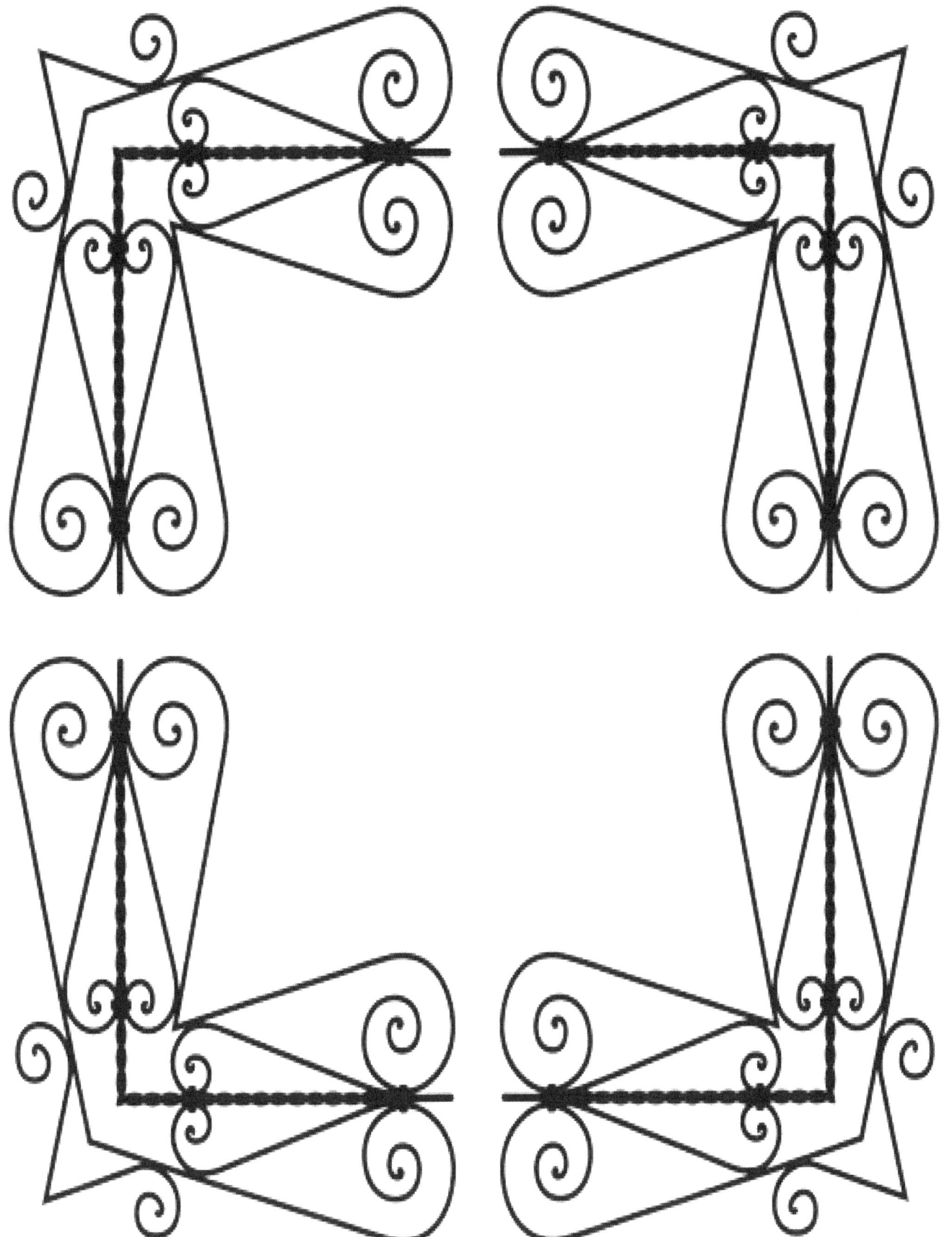

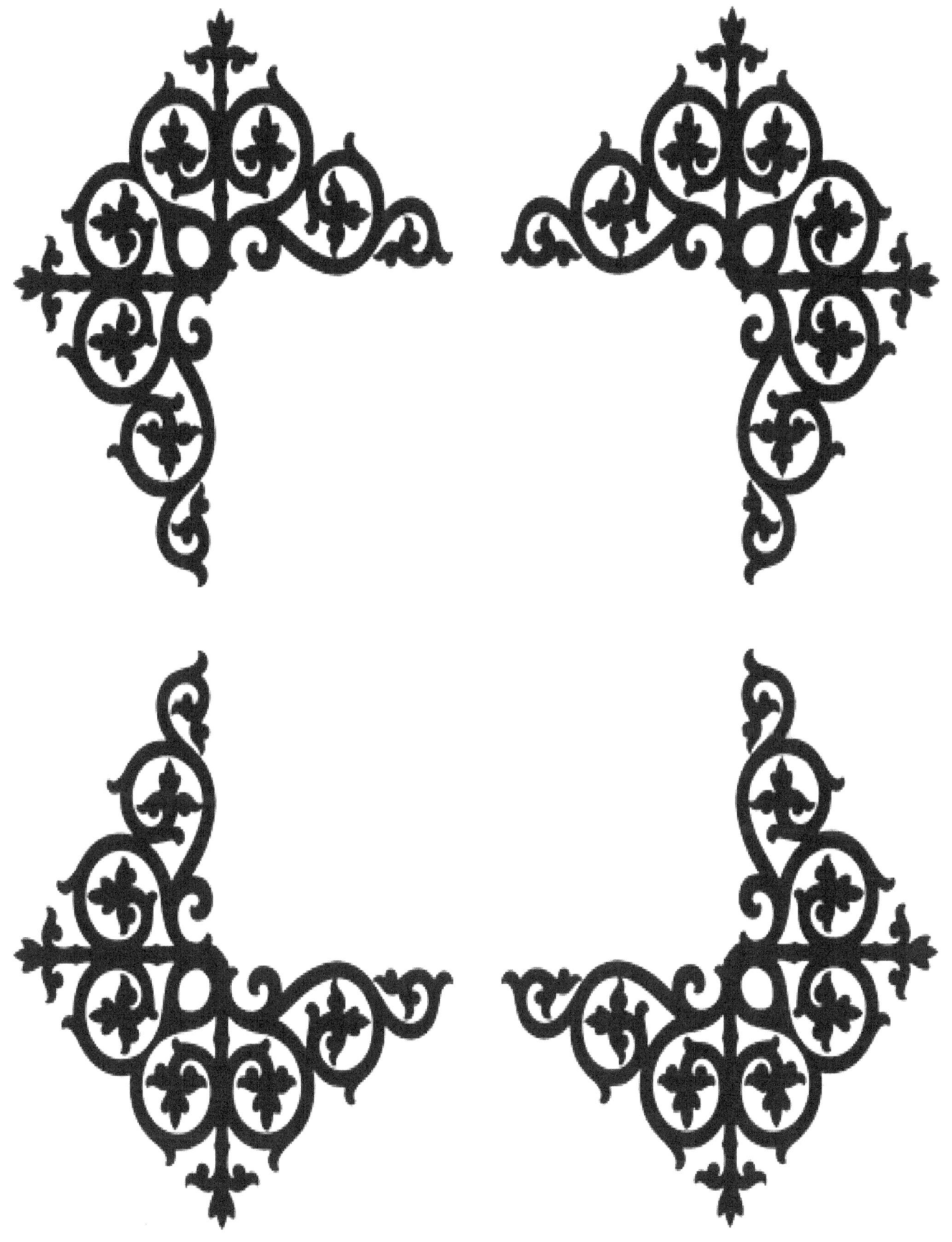

blank page for bleed

Blank for bleed

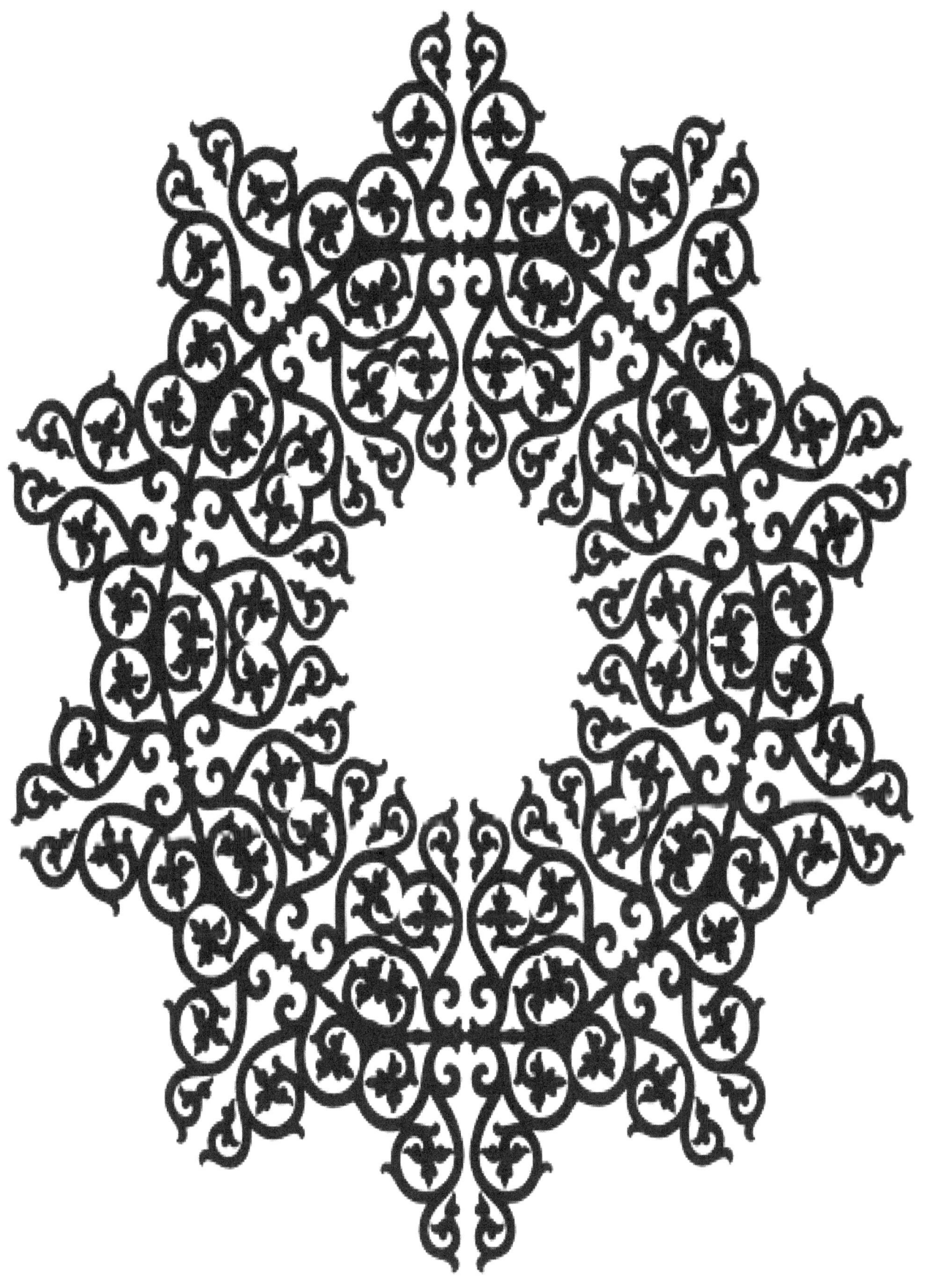

Blank for bleed

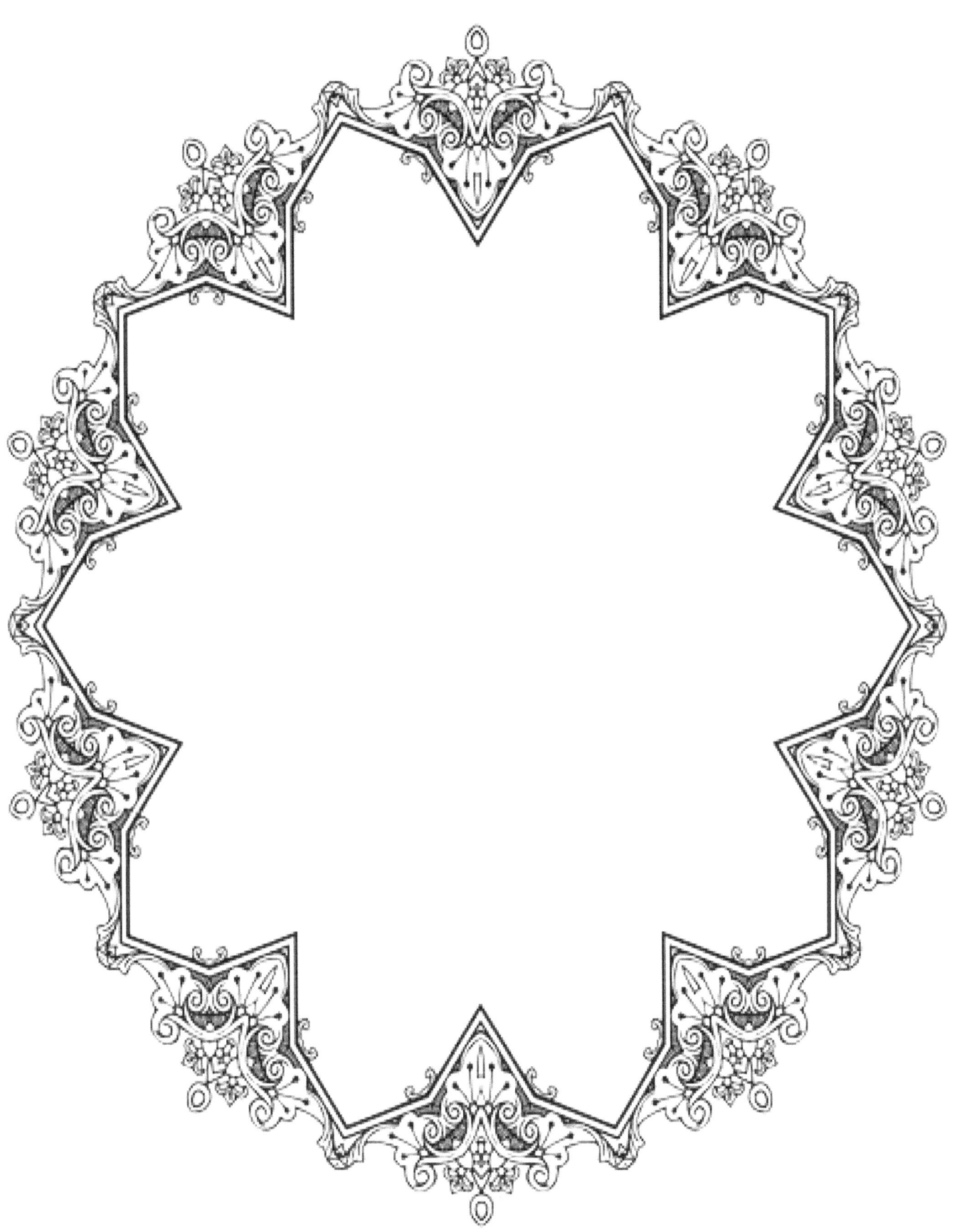

blank for bleed

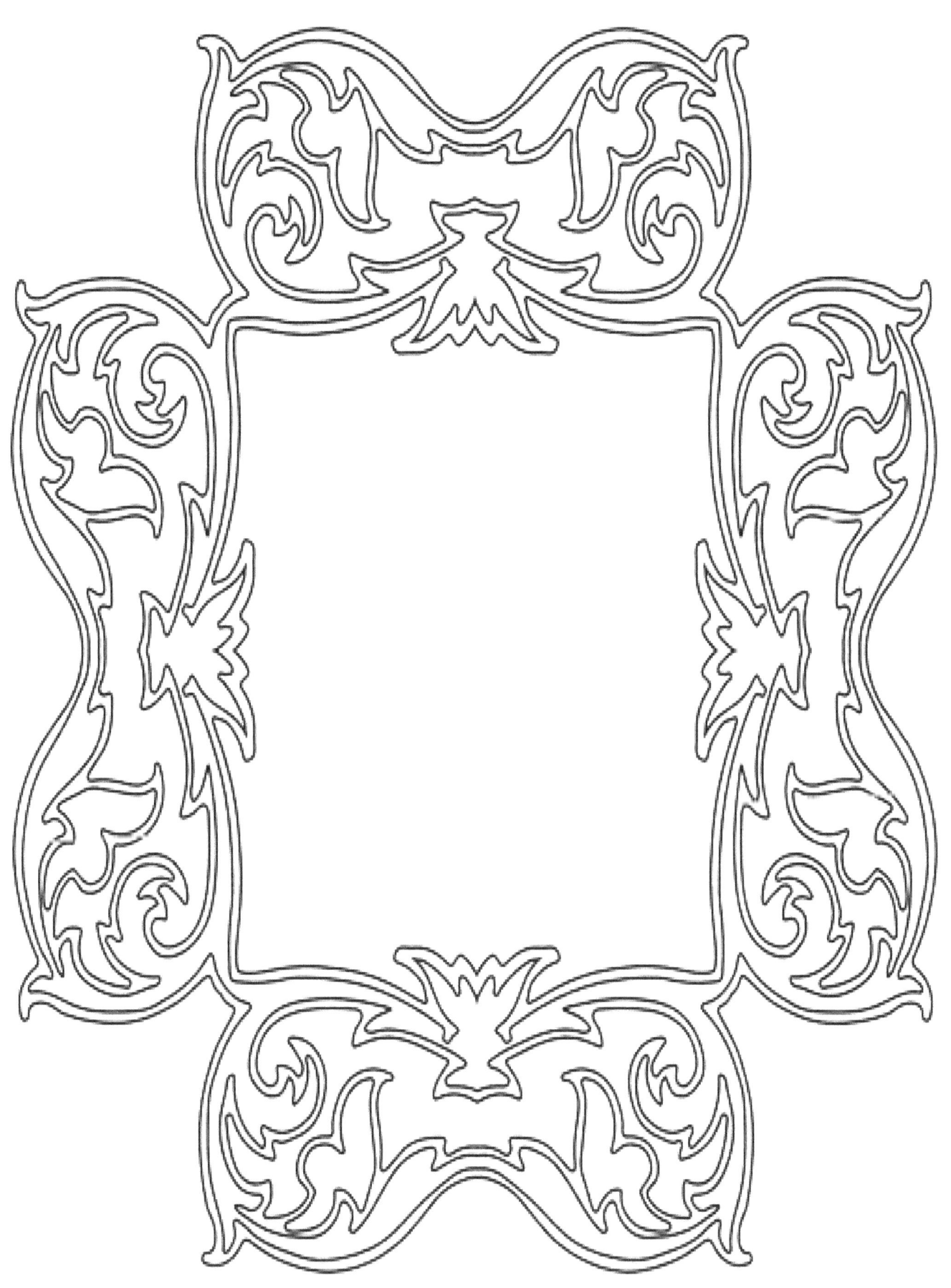

Blank for bleed

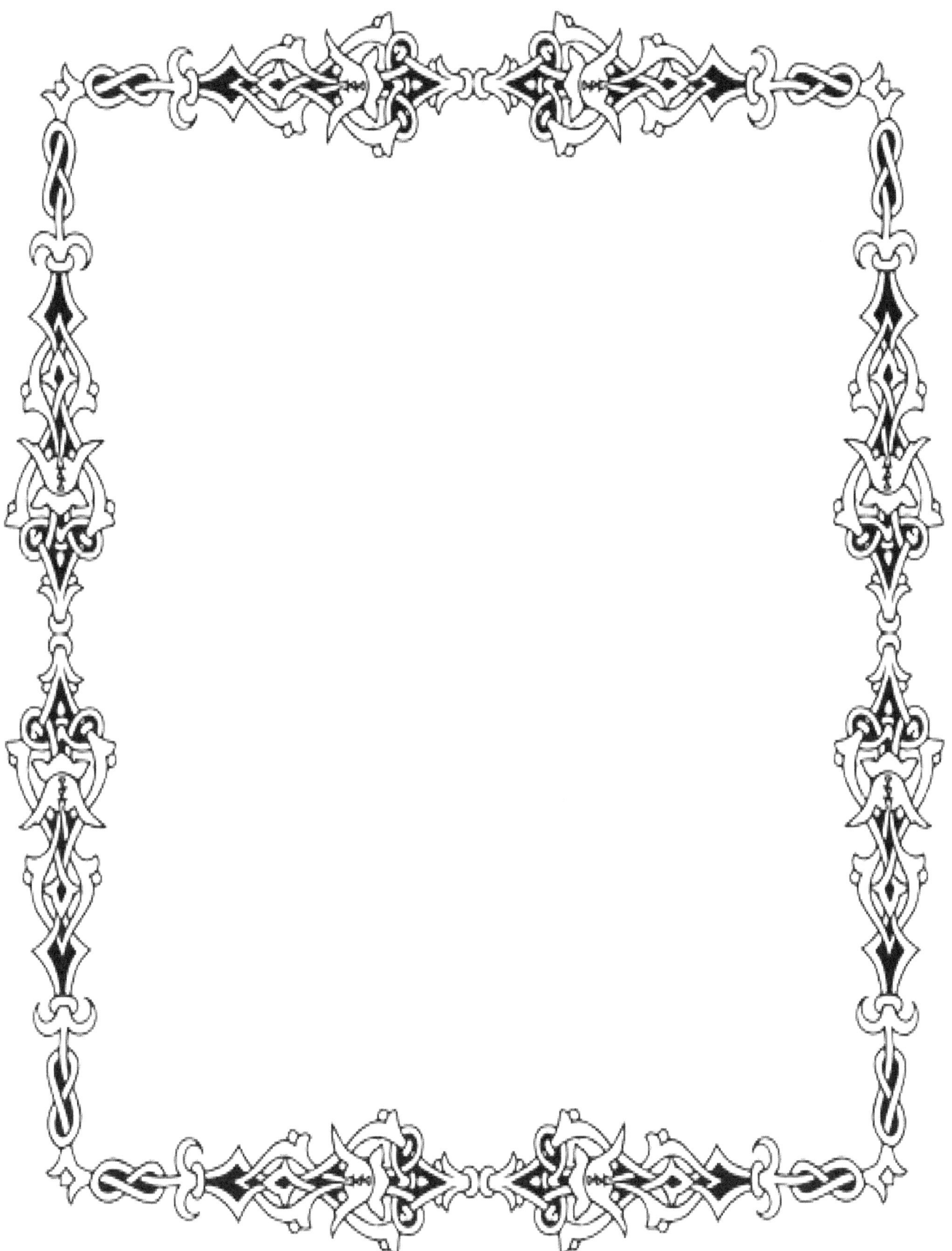

Blank for bleed

Blank for bleed

Blank for bleed

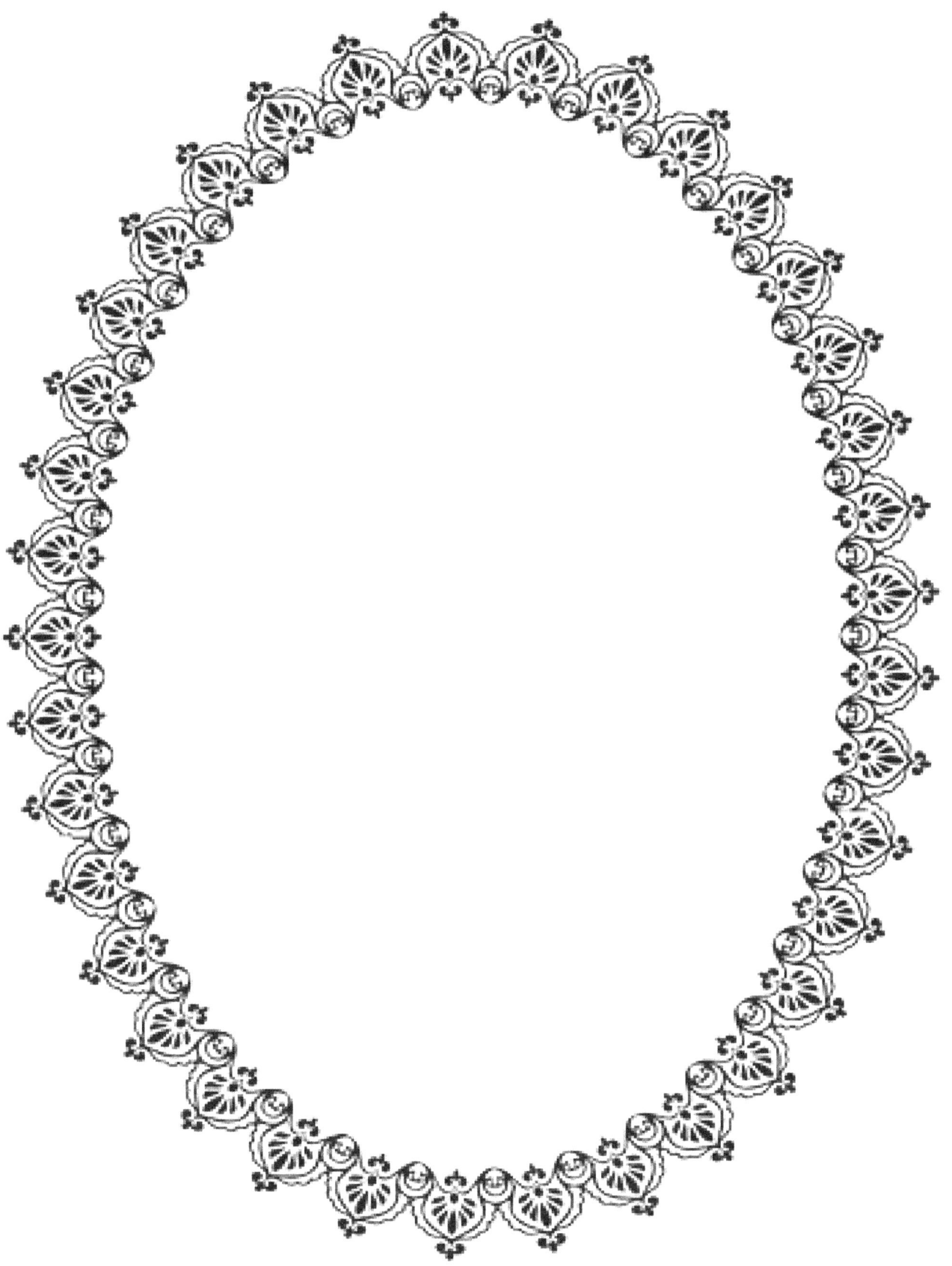

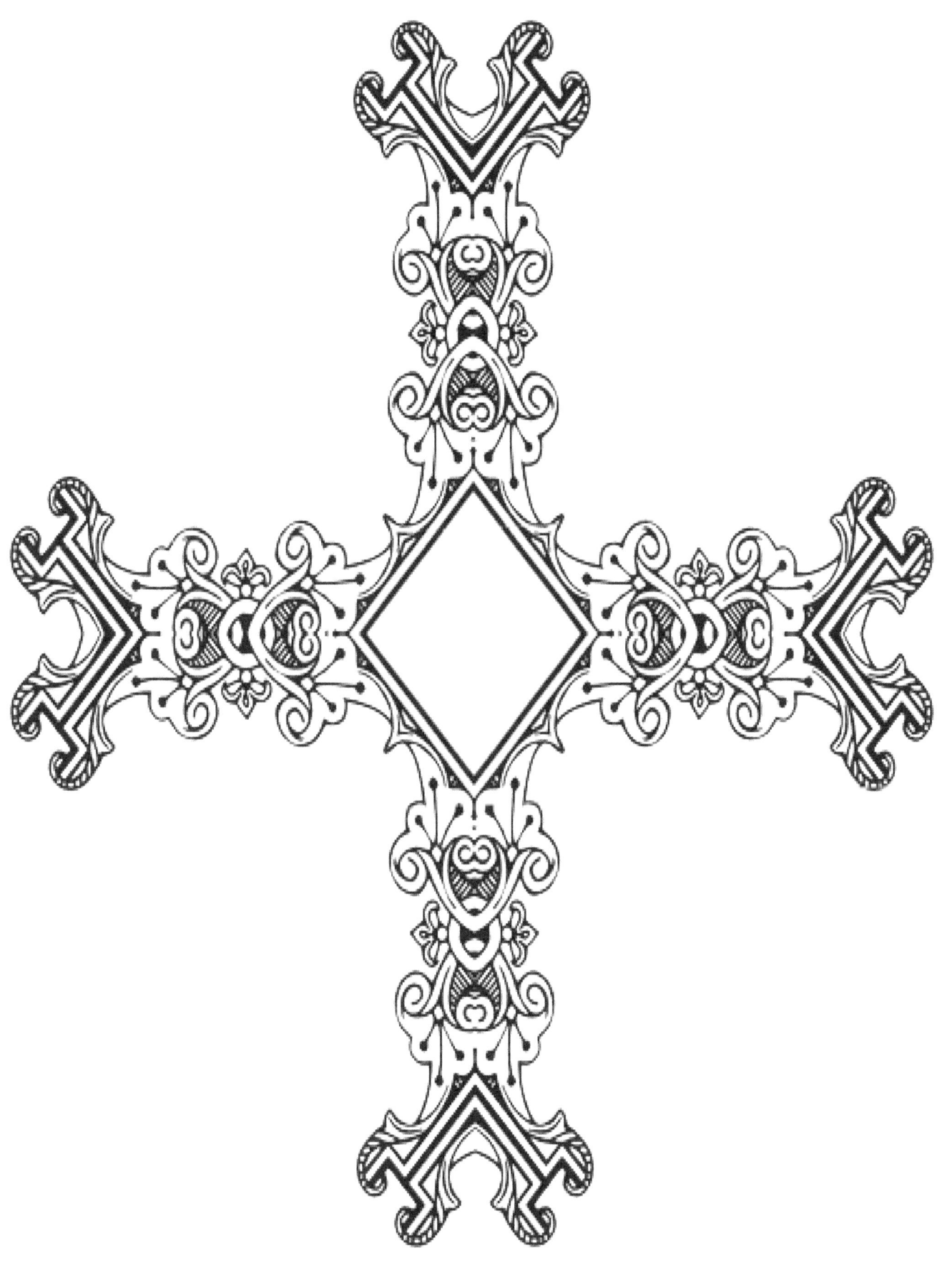

Blank for bleed

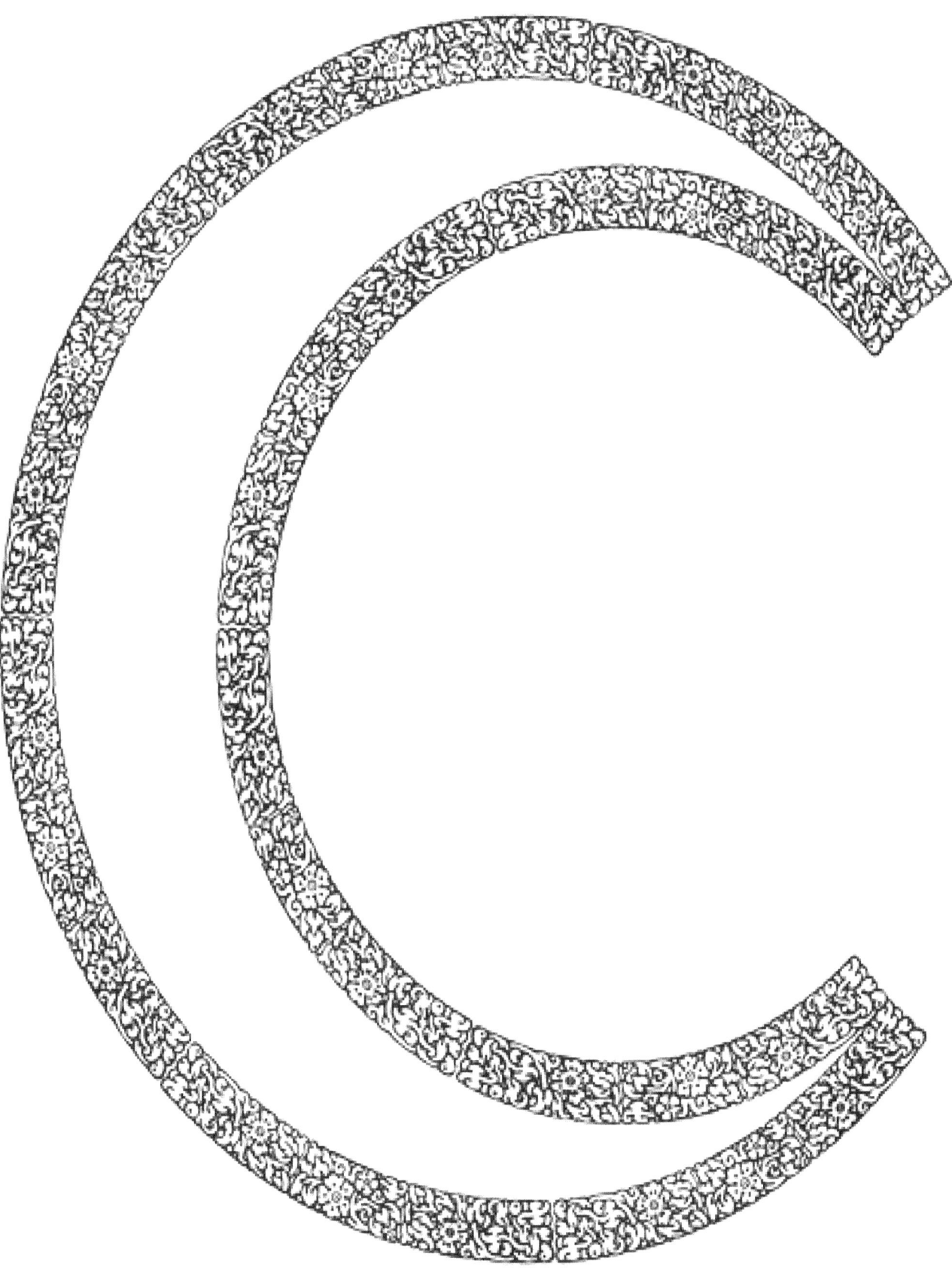

blank for bleed

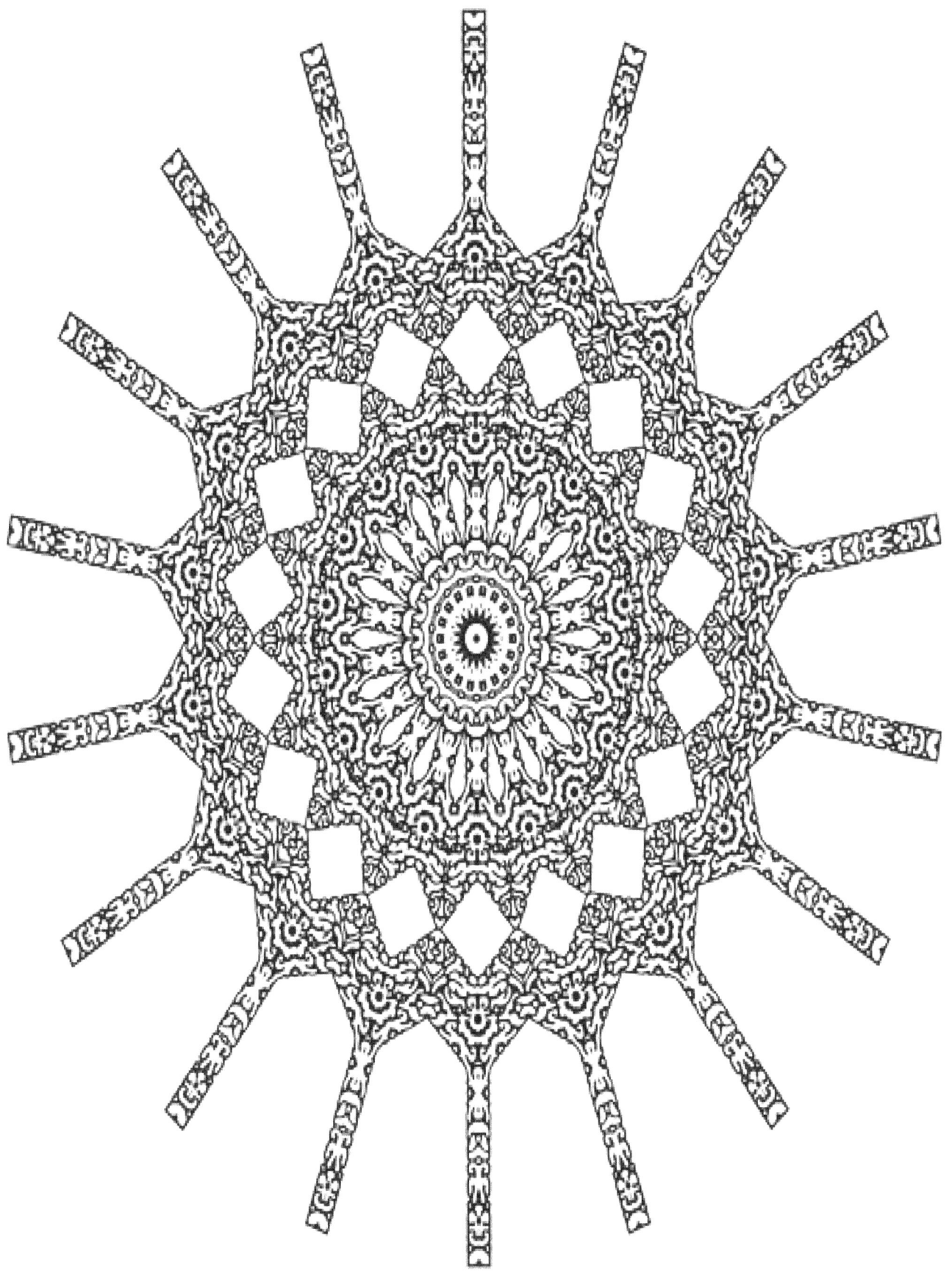

Blank for bleed

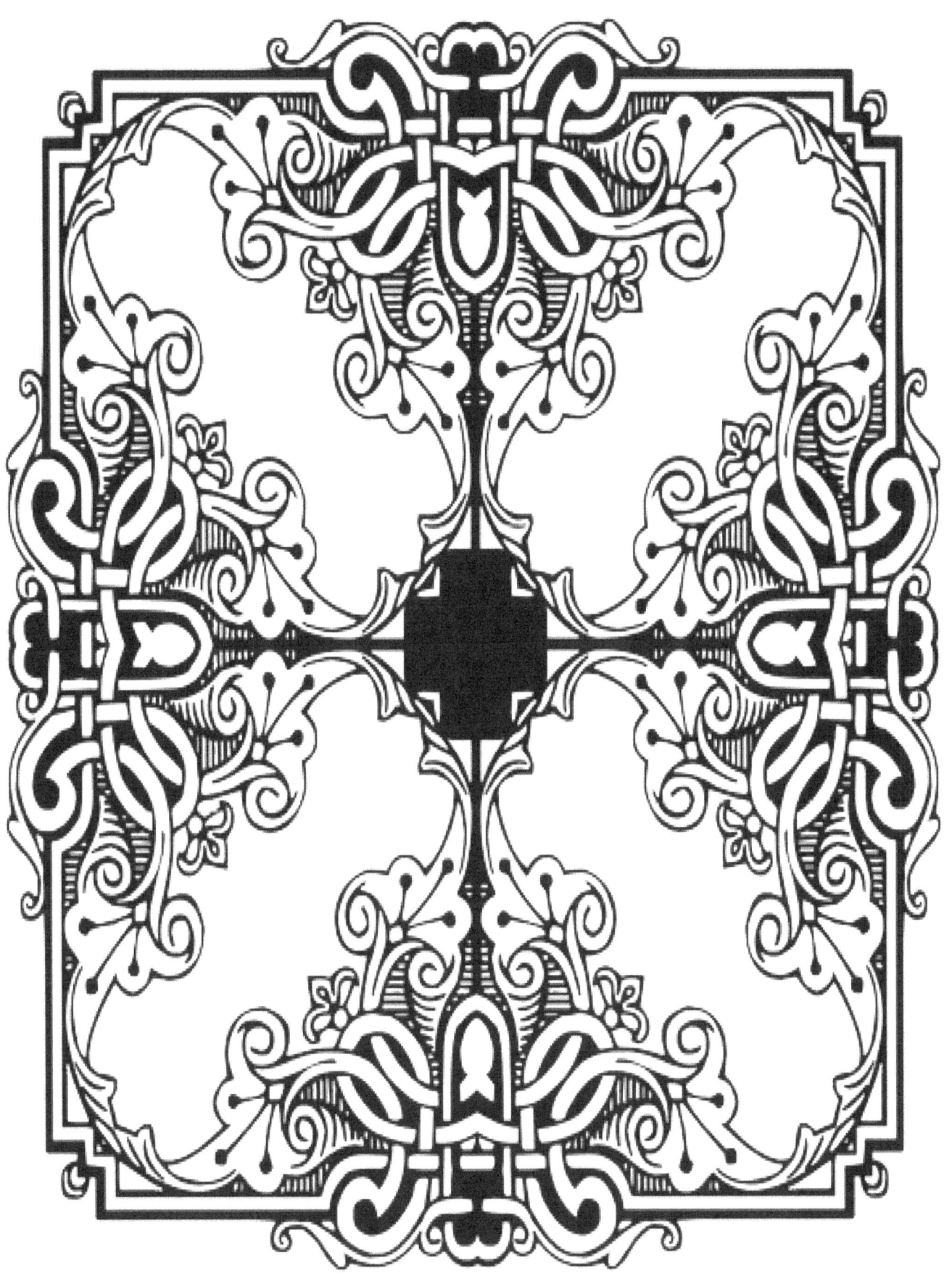

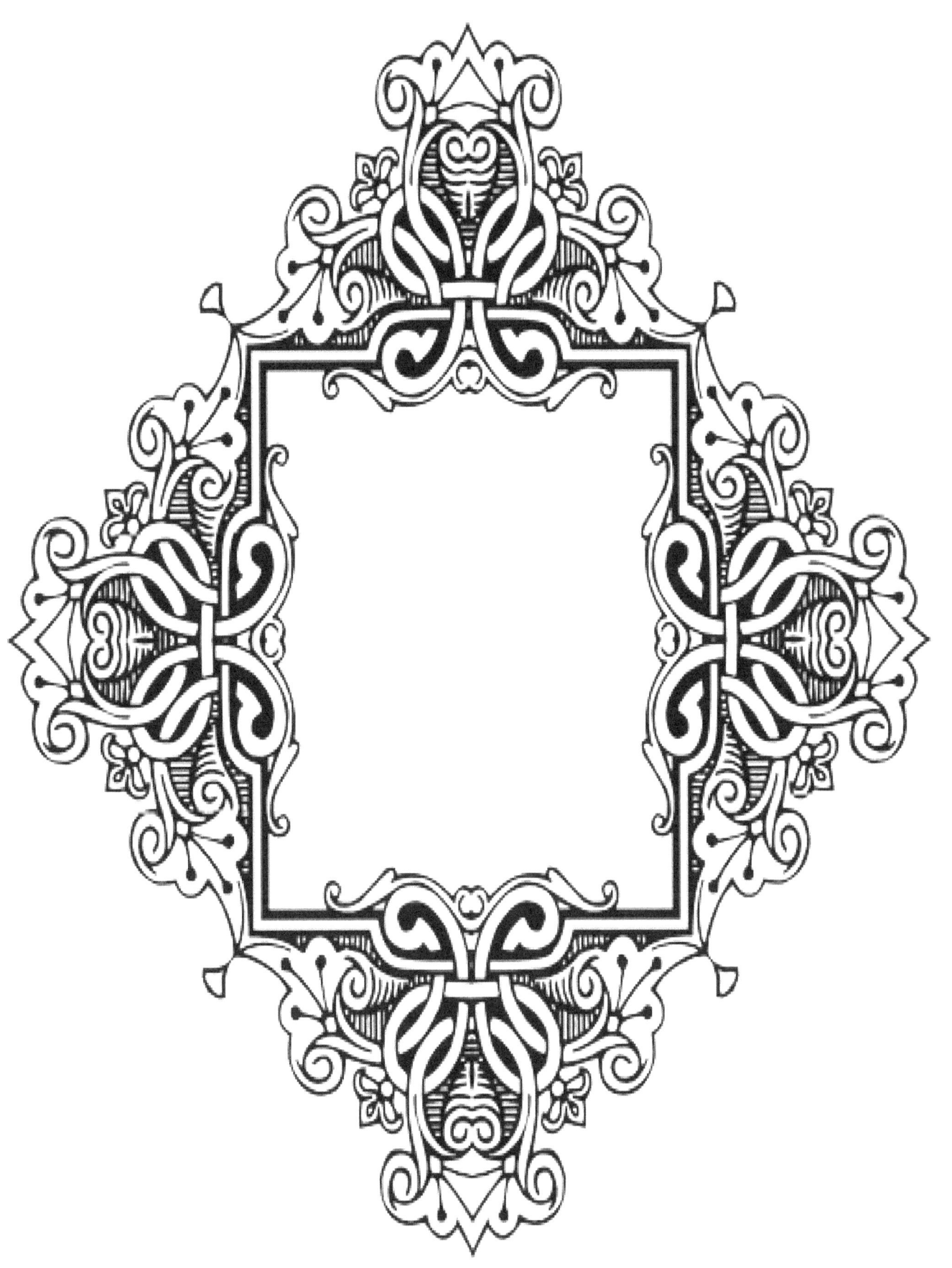

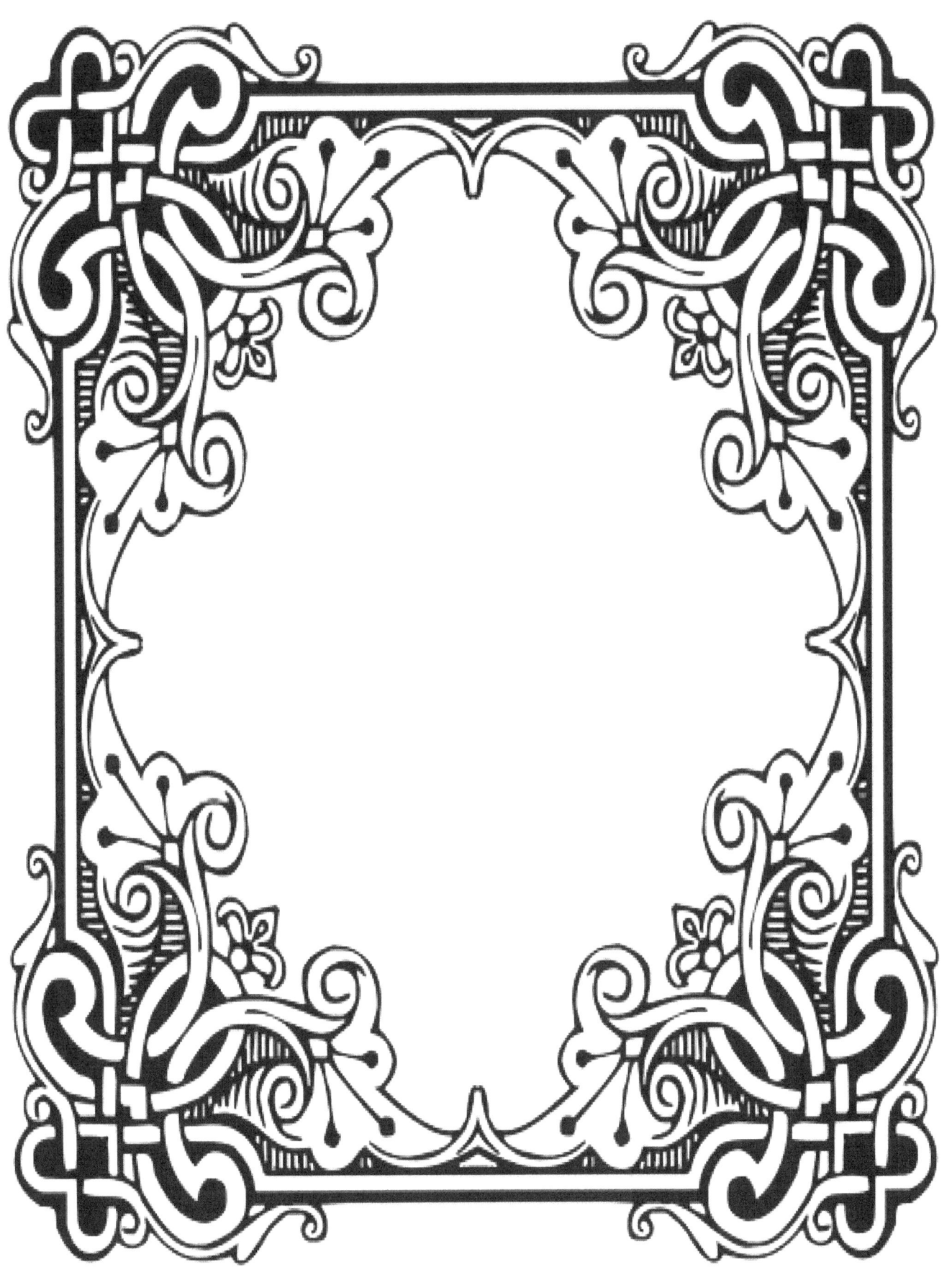

blank for bleed

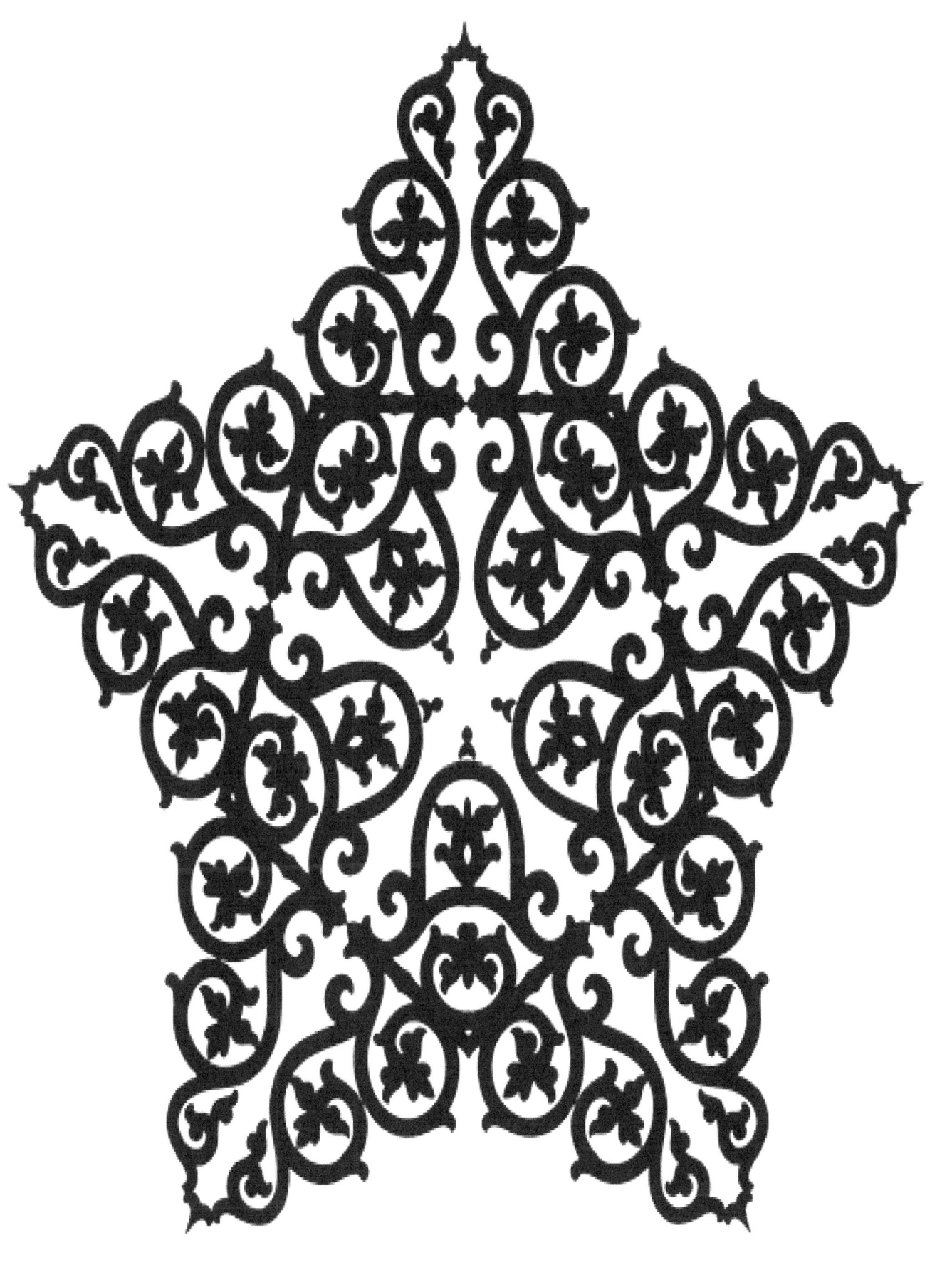

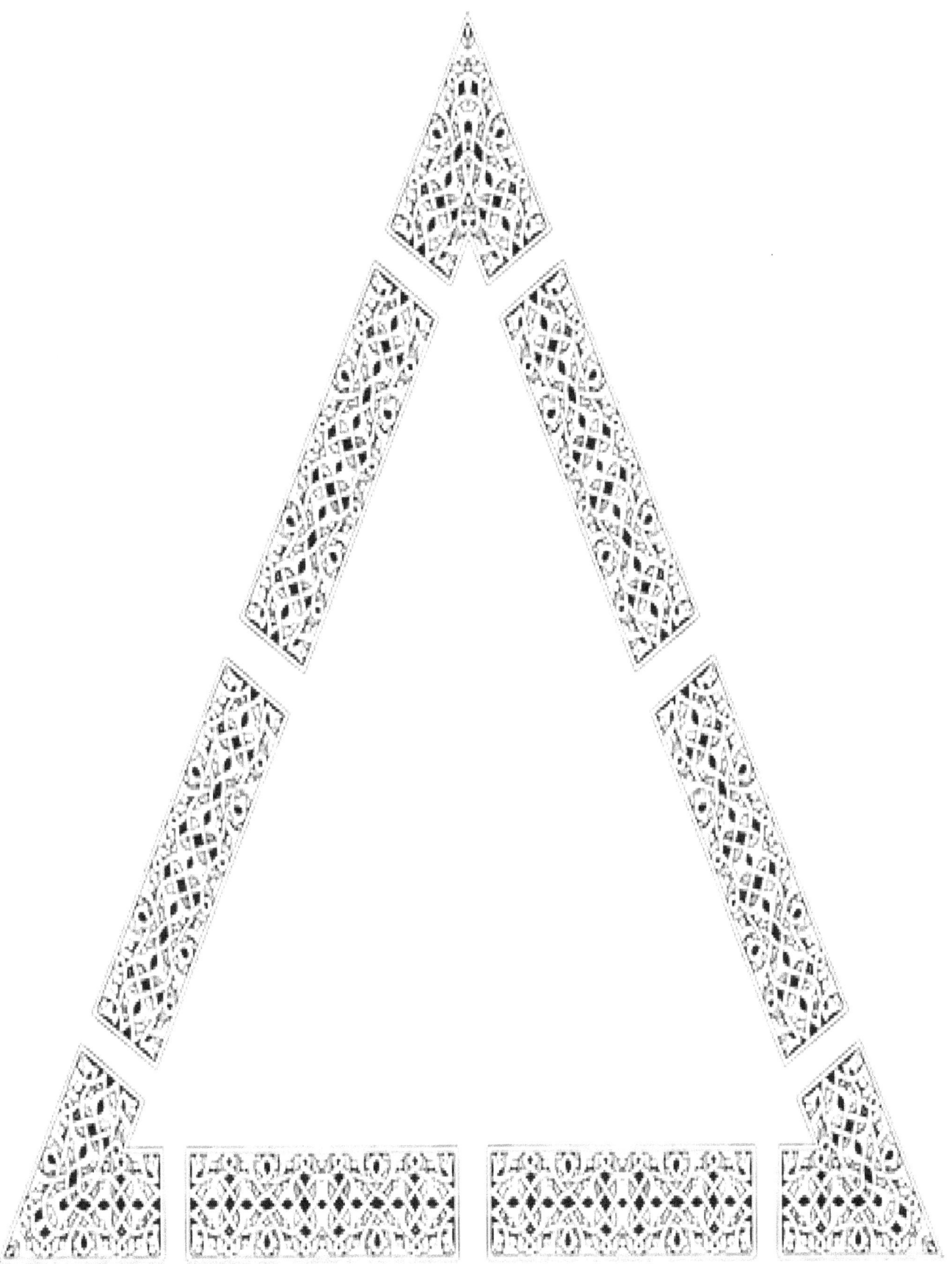

Blank for bleed

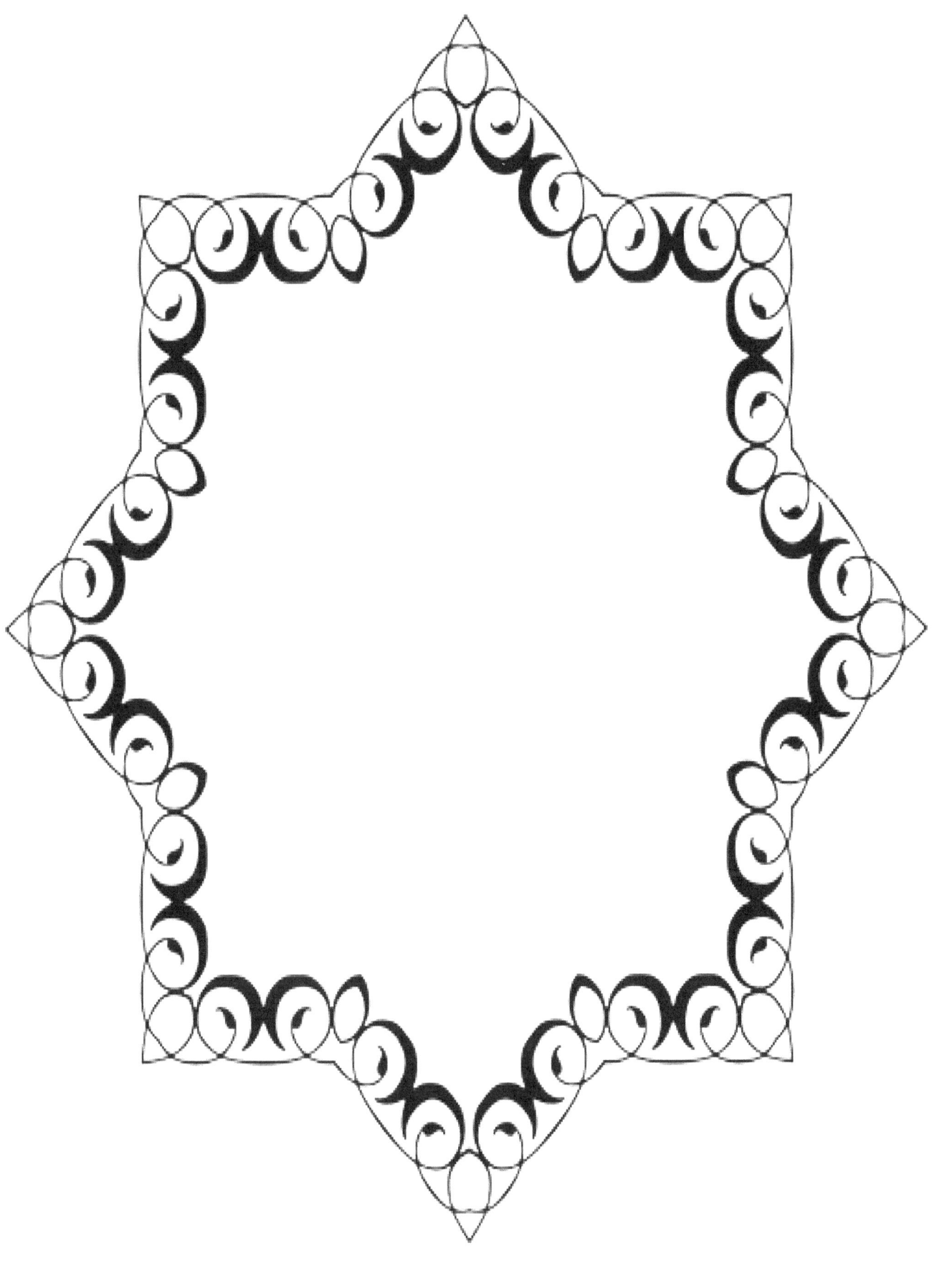

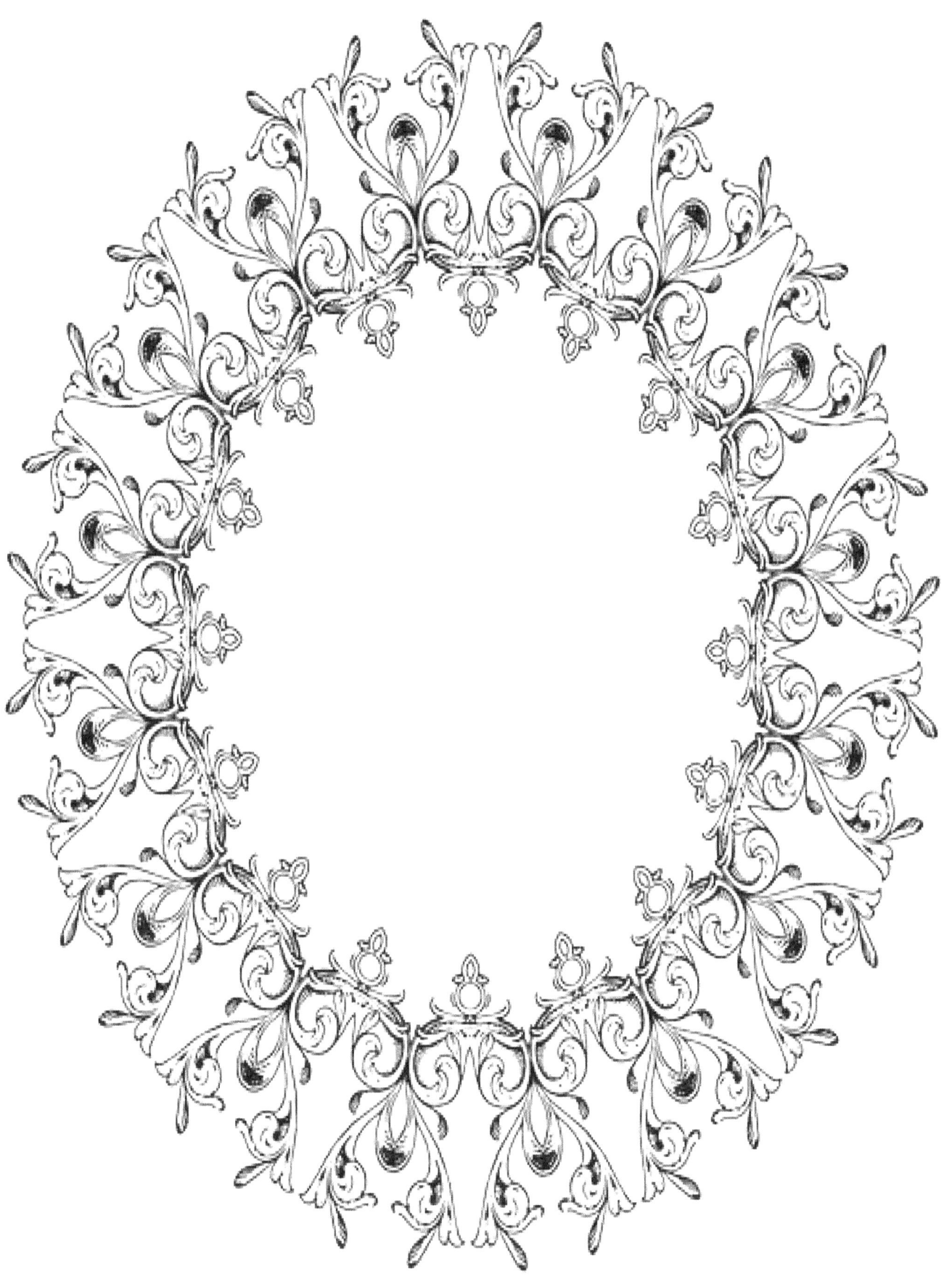

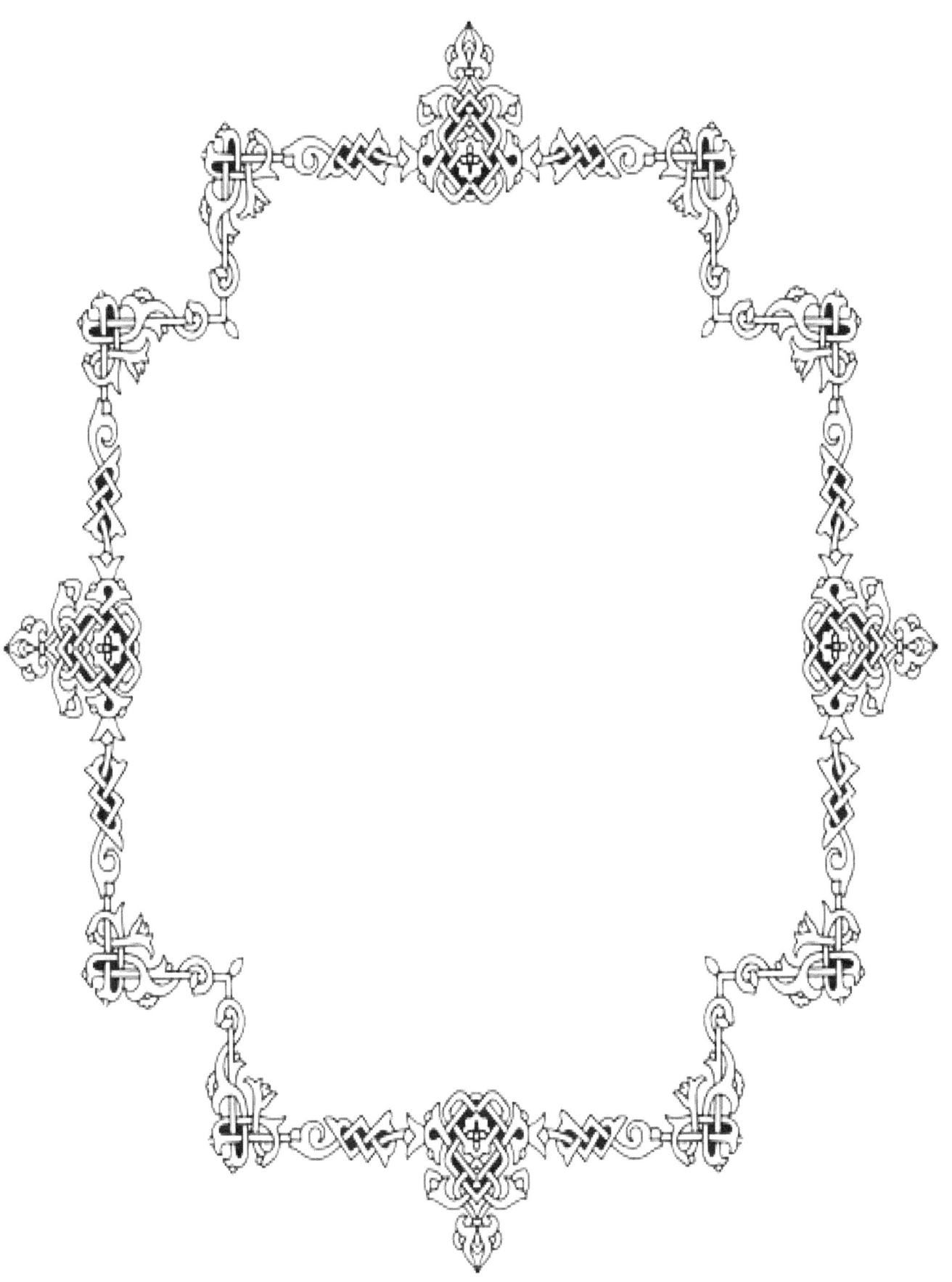

blank for bleed

Blank for bleed

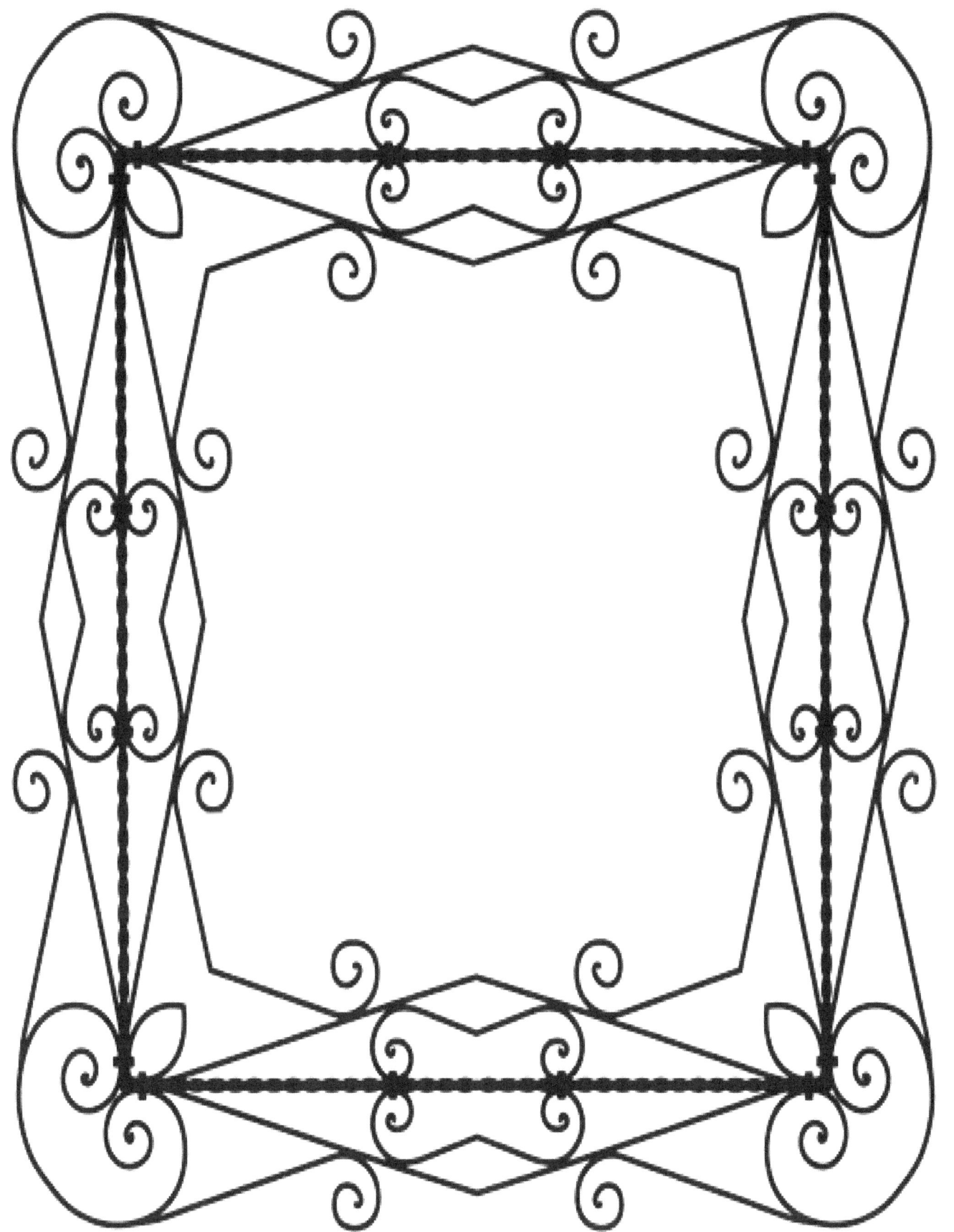

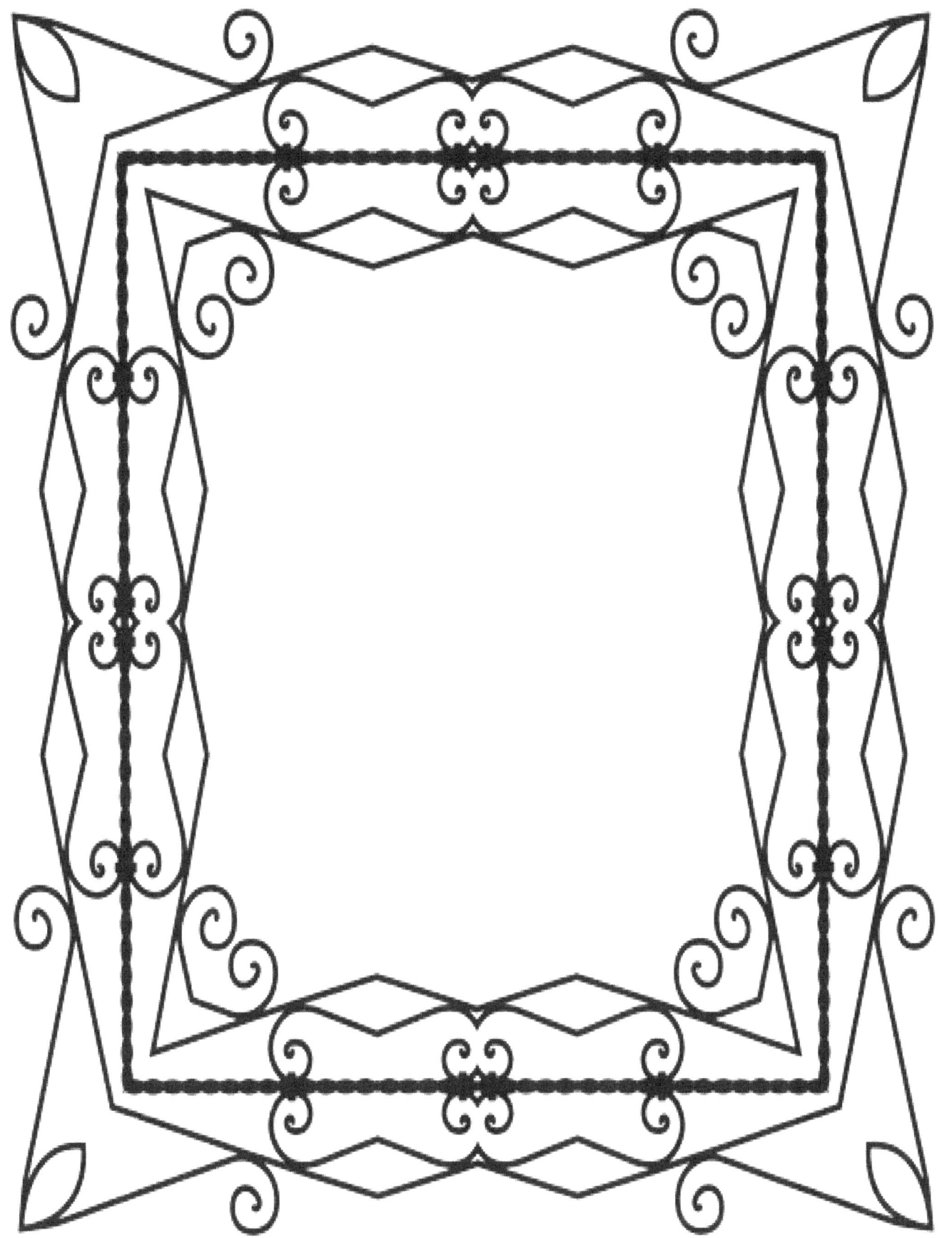

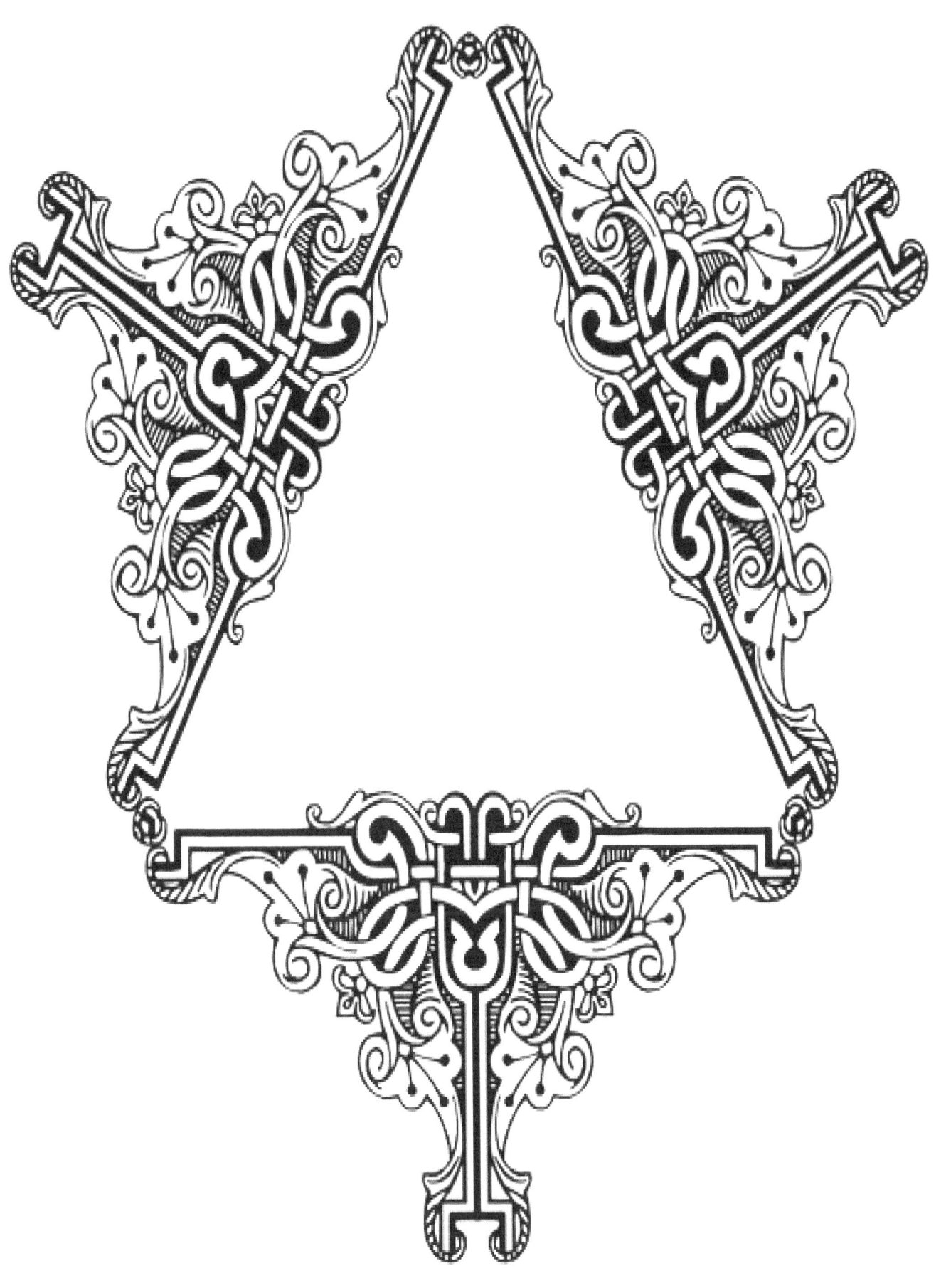

Blank for bleed

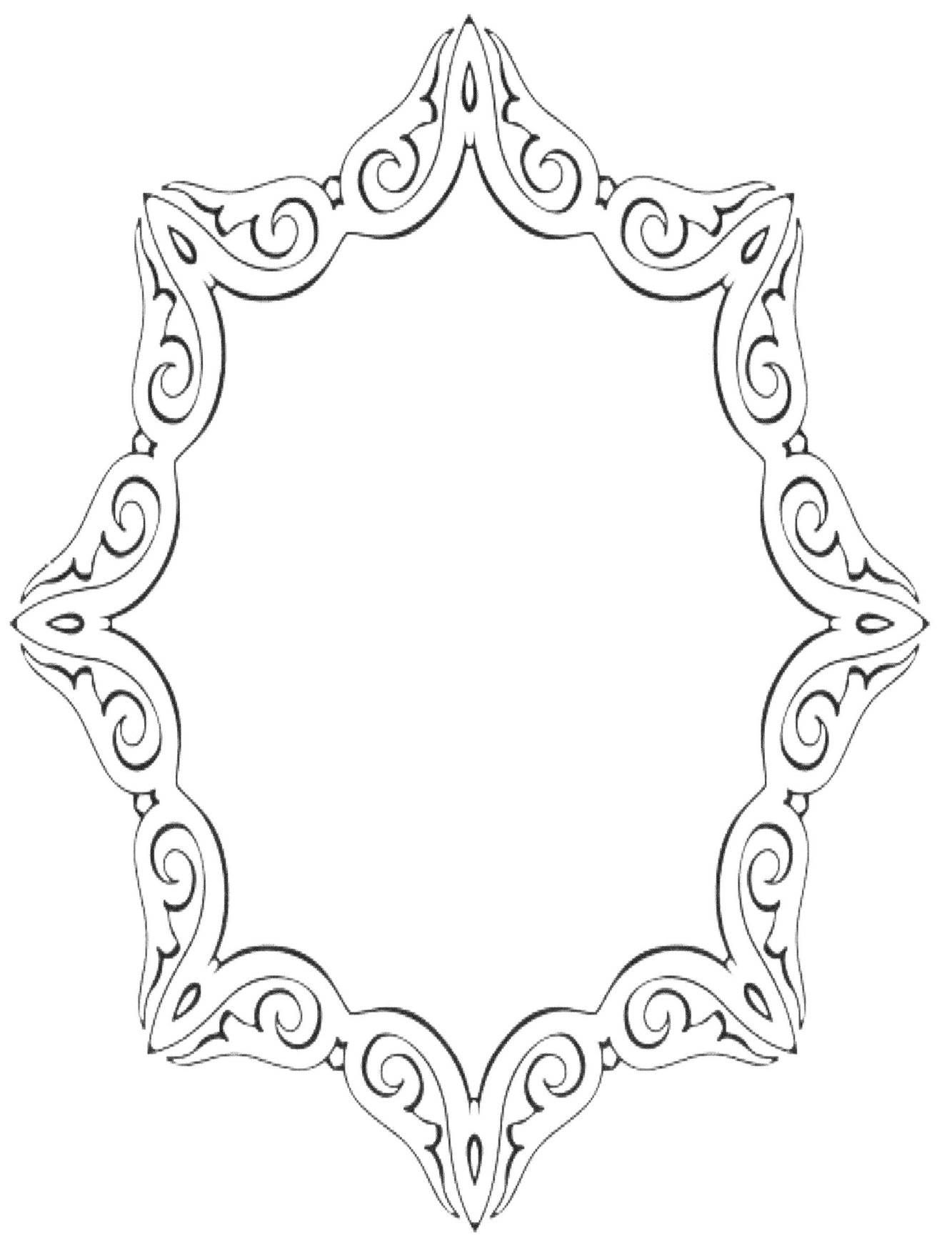

Blank for bleed

Blank for bleed

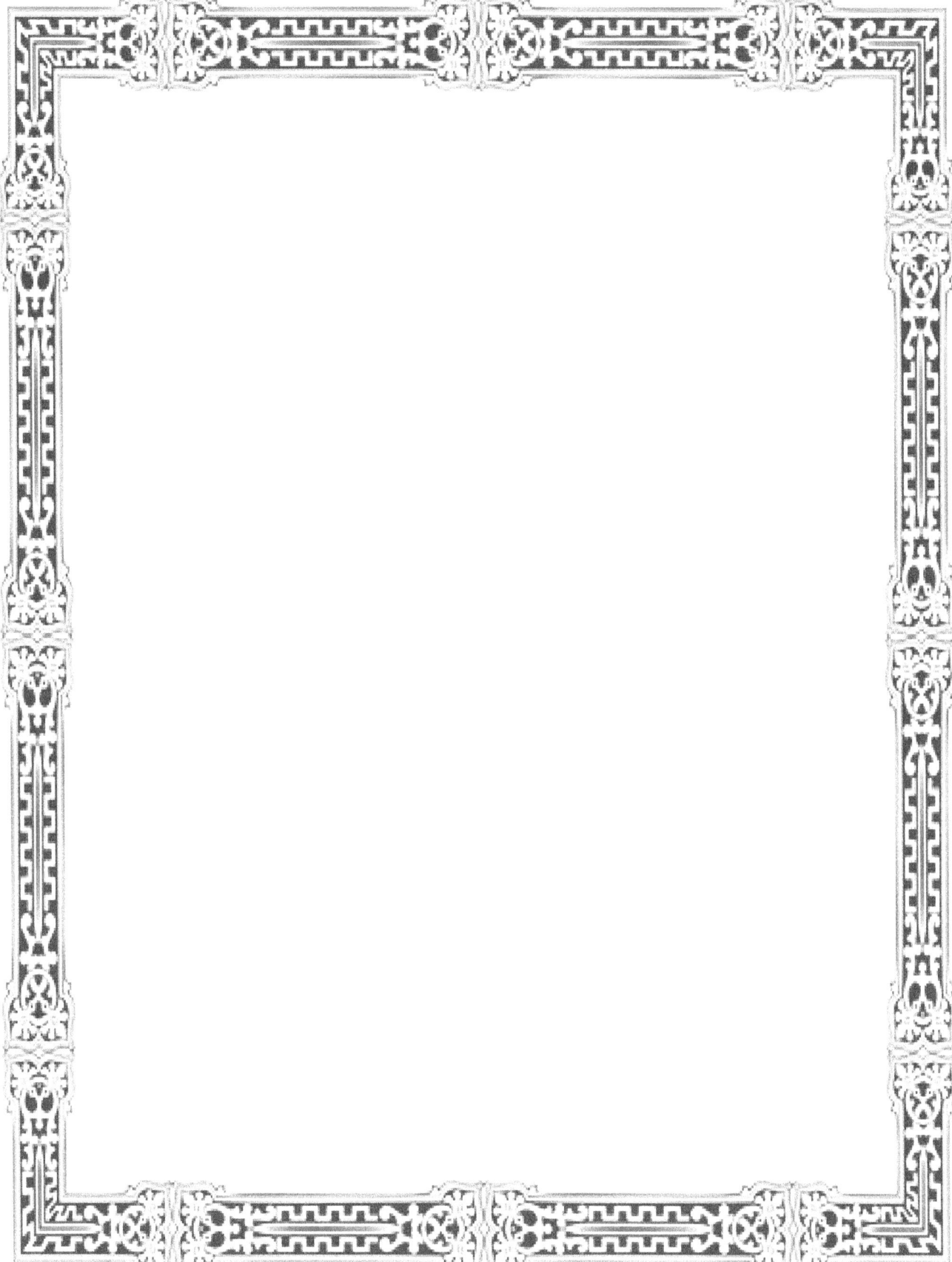

Blank for bleed

Blank for bleed

blank for bleed

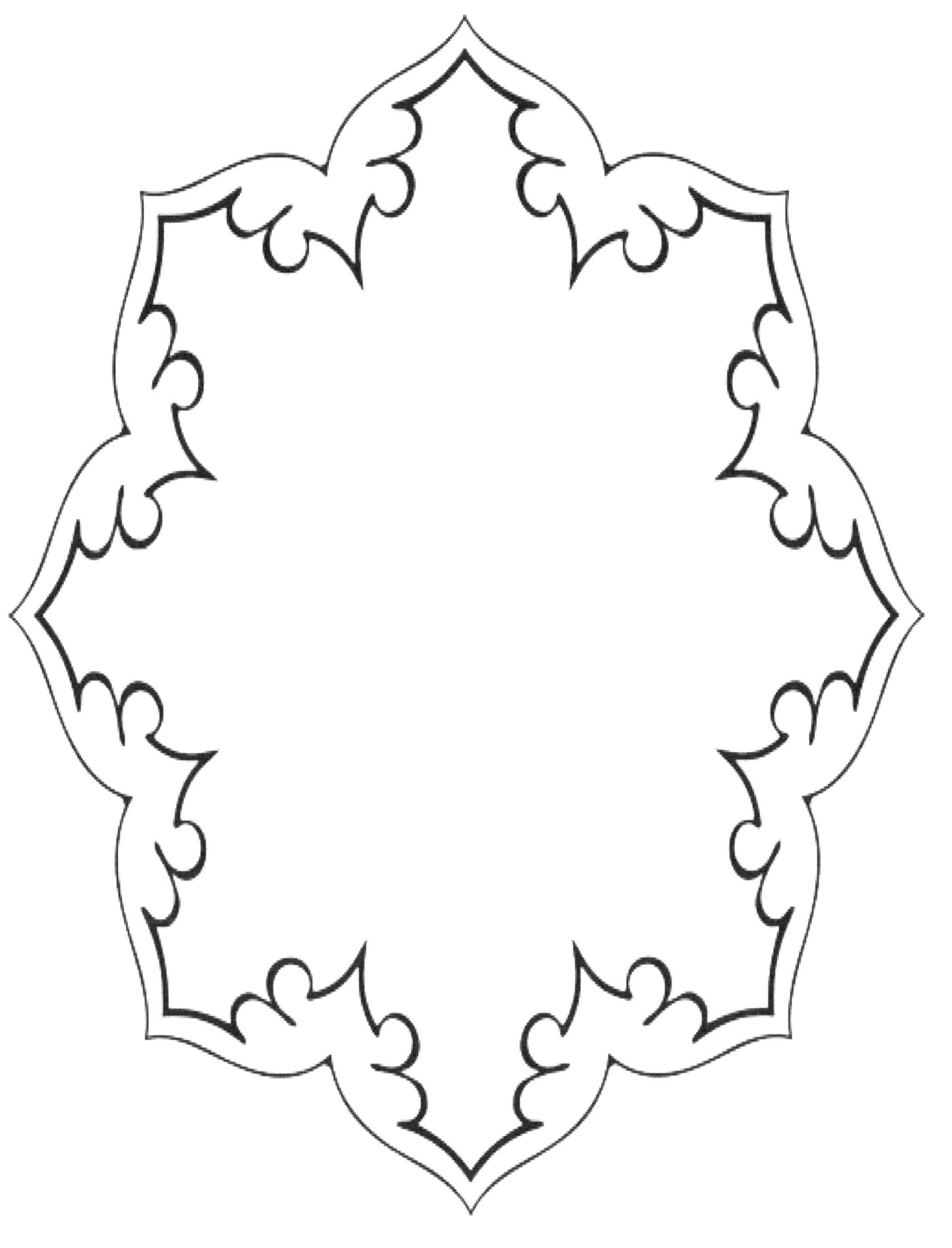

blank for bleed

Blank for bleed

Blank for bleed

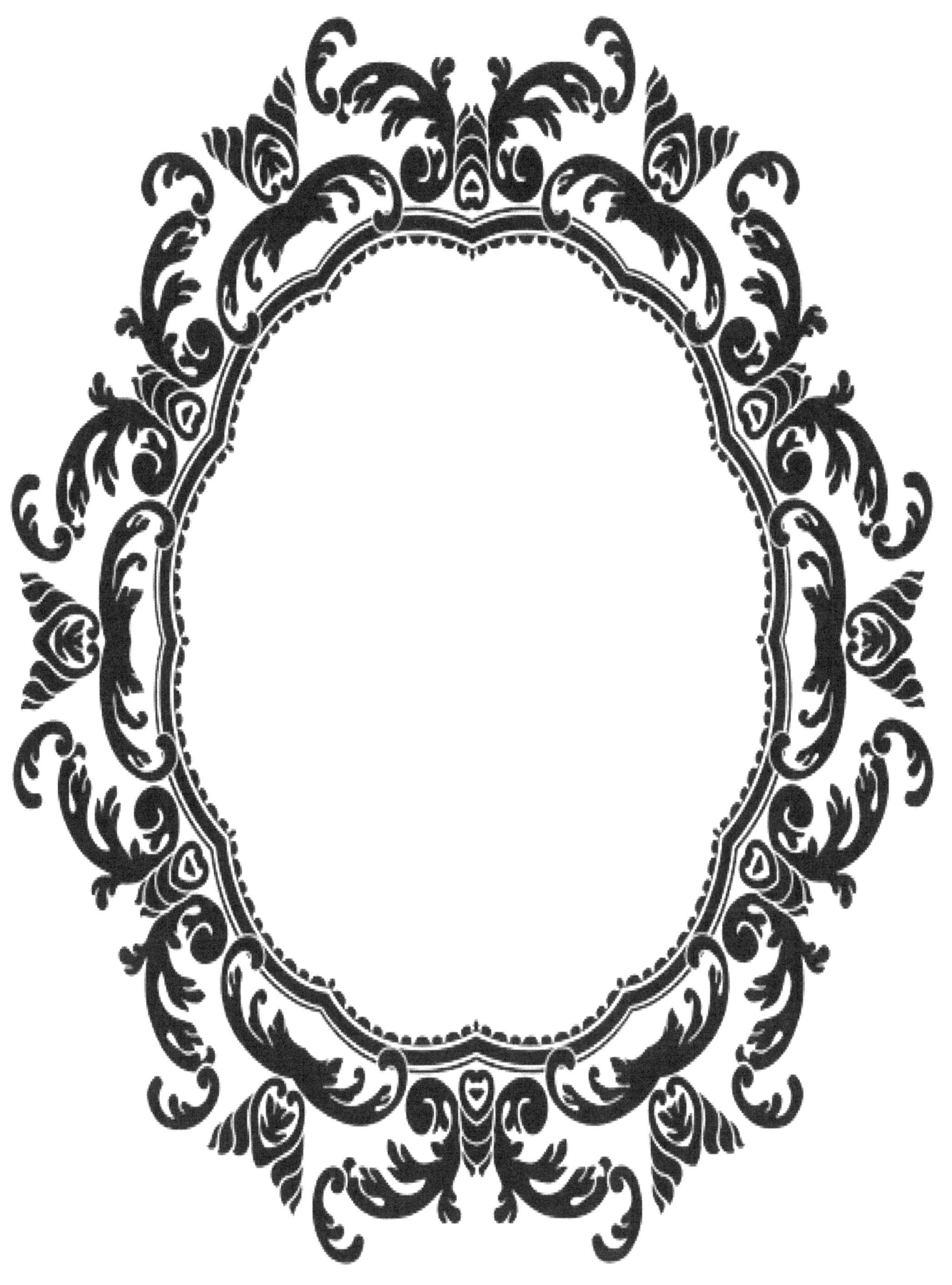

Blank for bleed

Blank for bleed

Blank for bleed

Blank for bleed

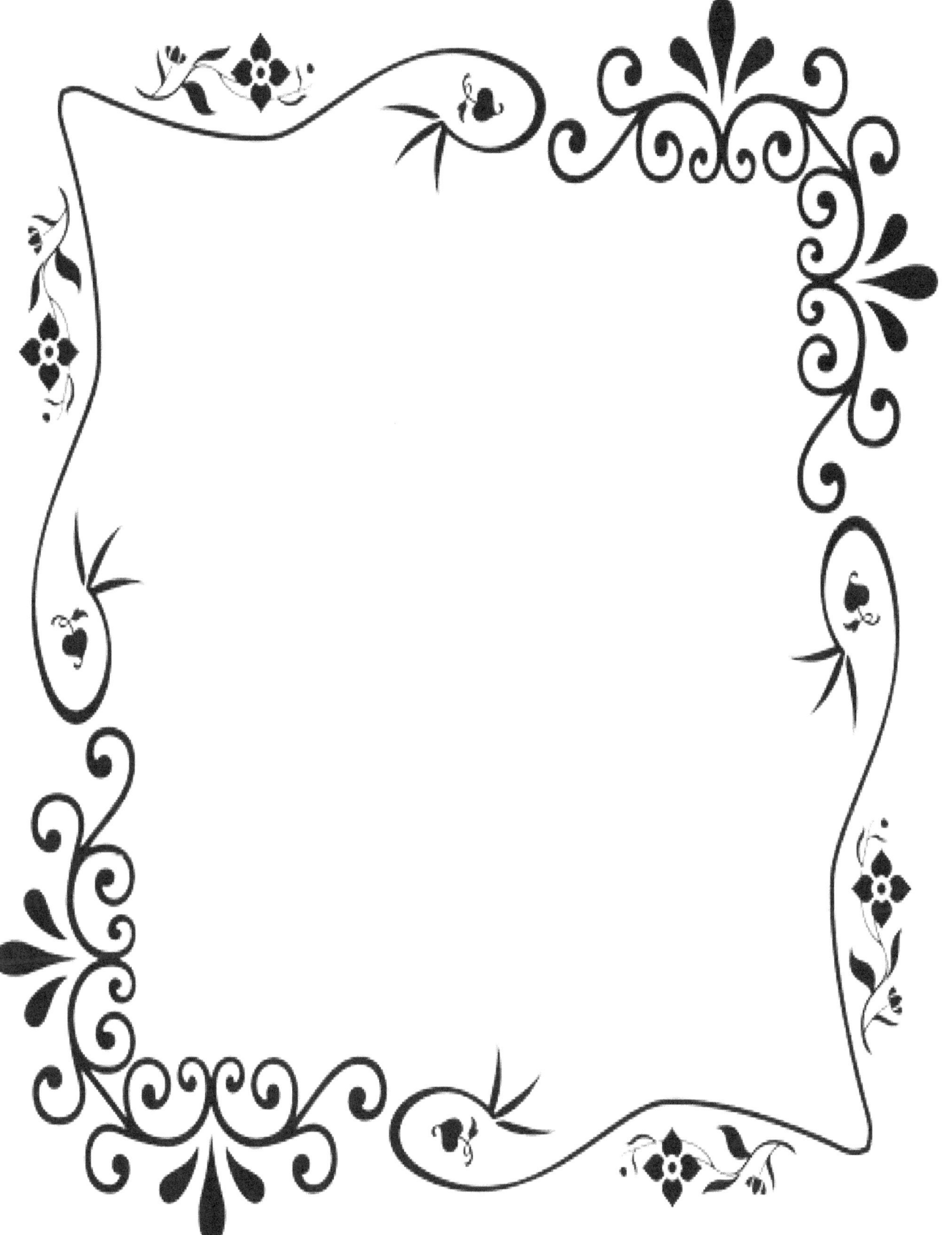

Blank for bleed

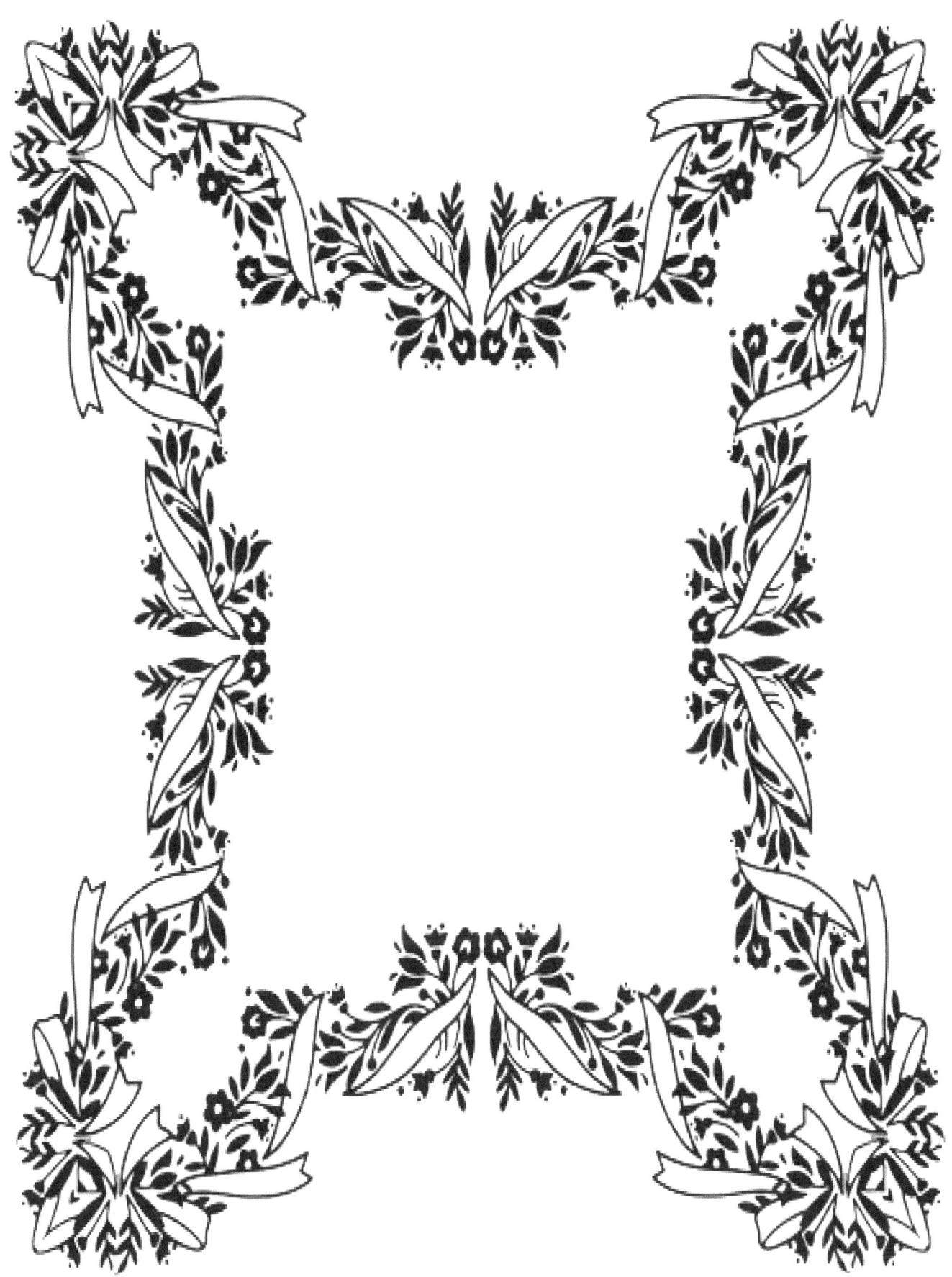

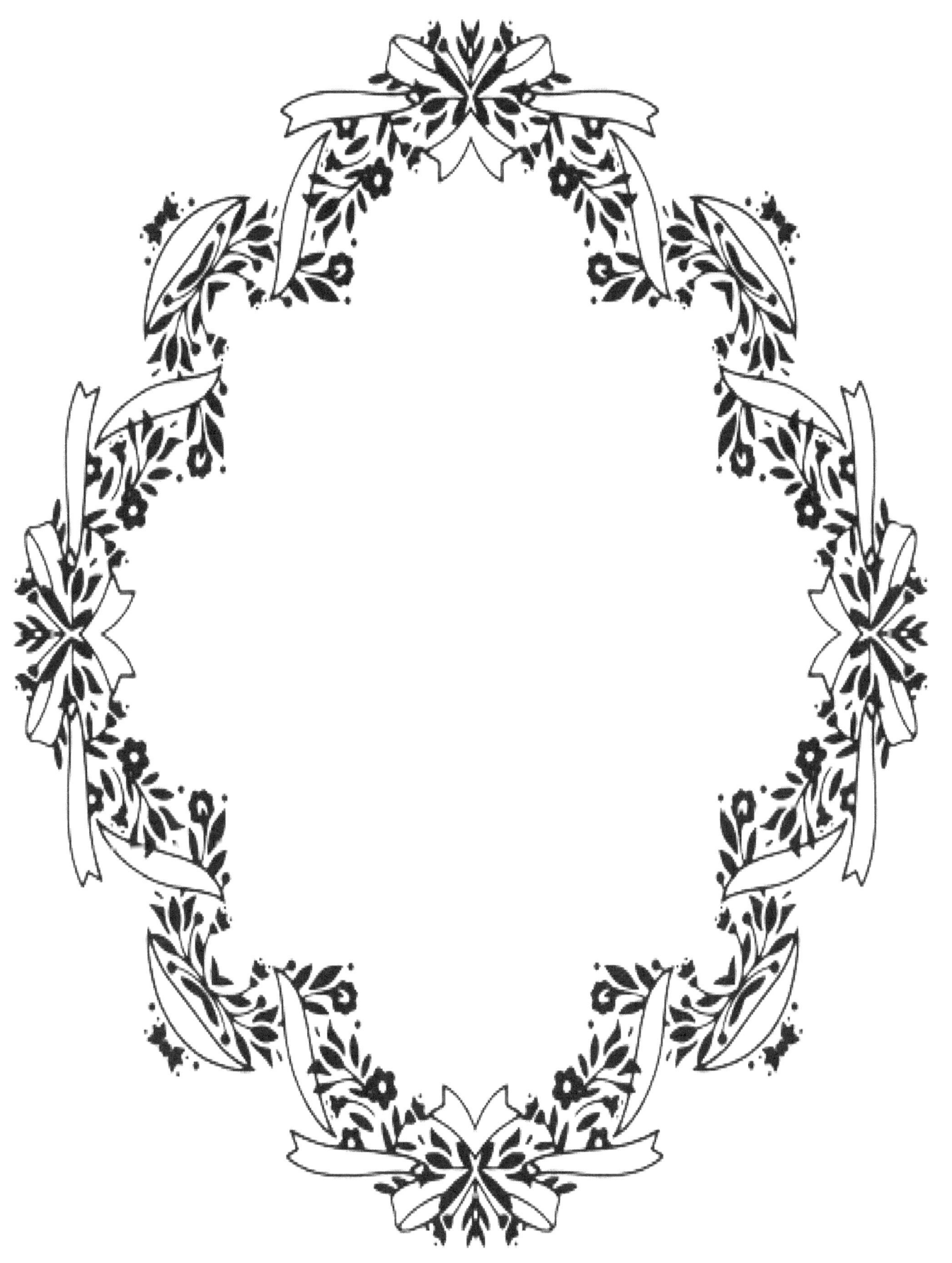

Blank for bleed

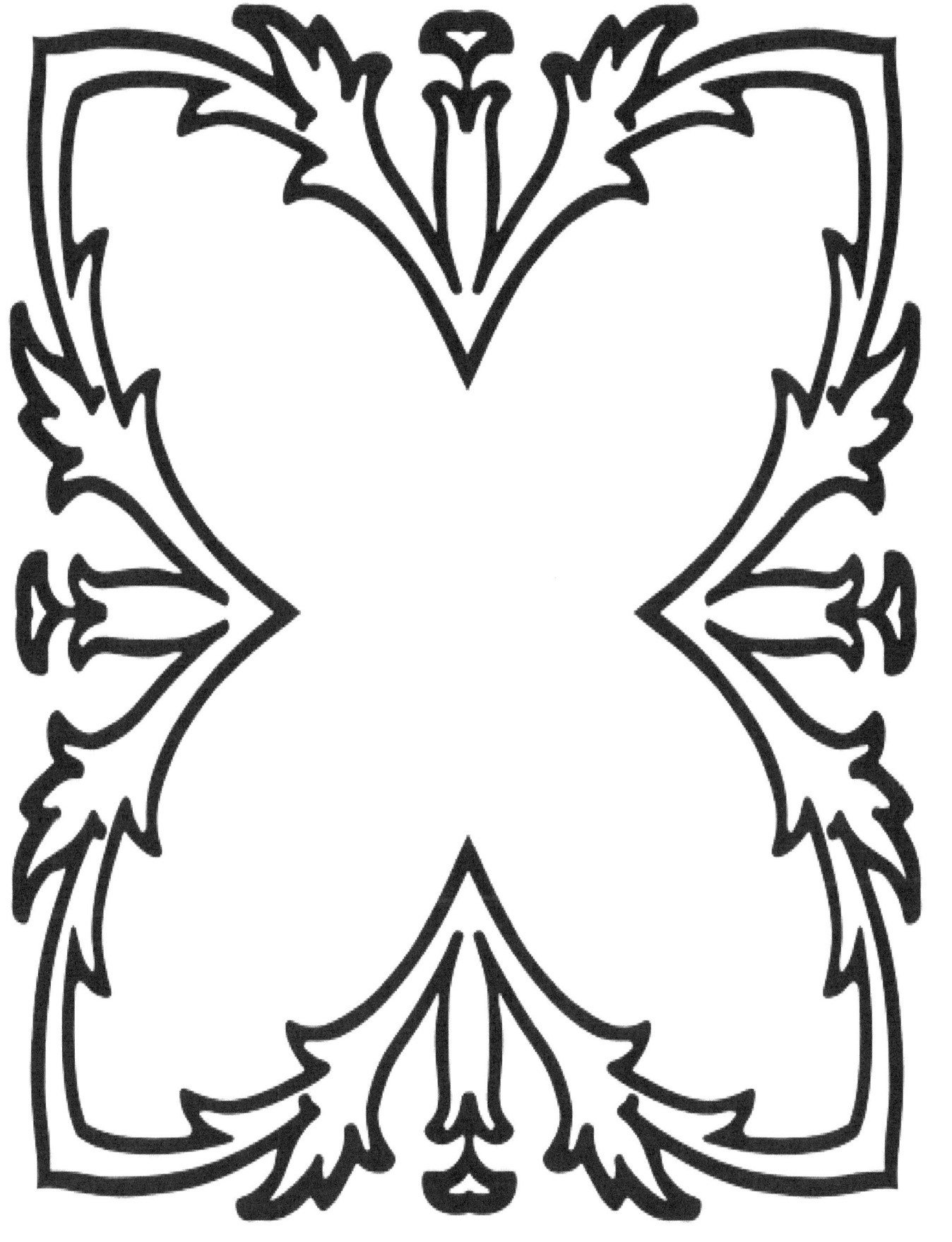

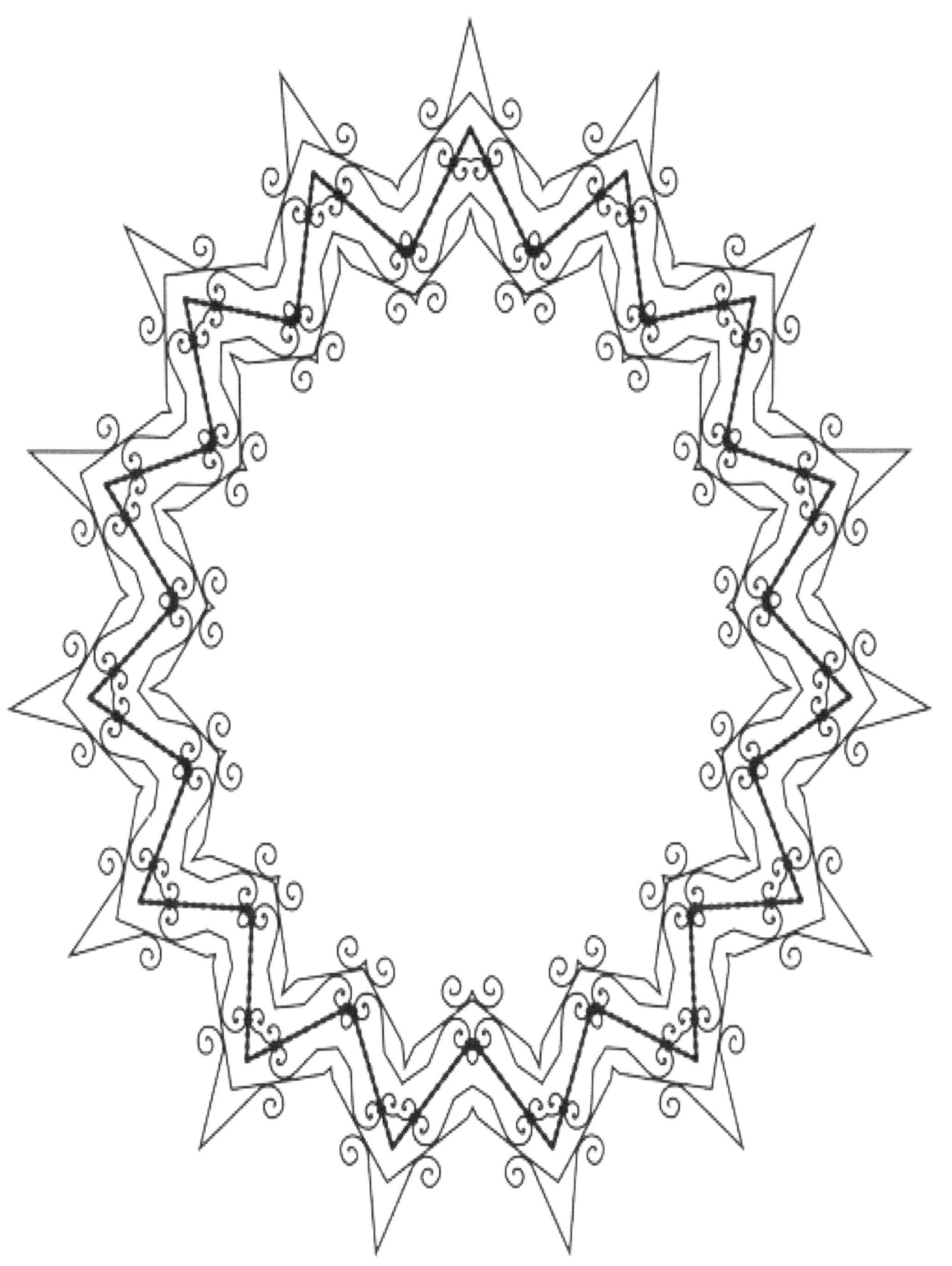

blank for bleed

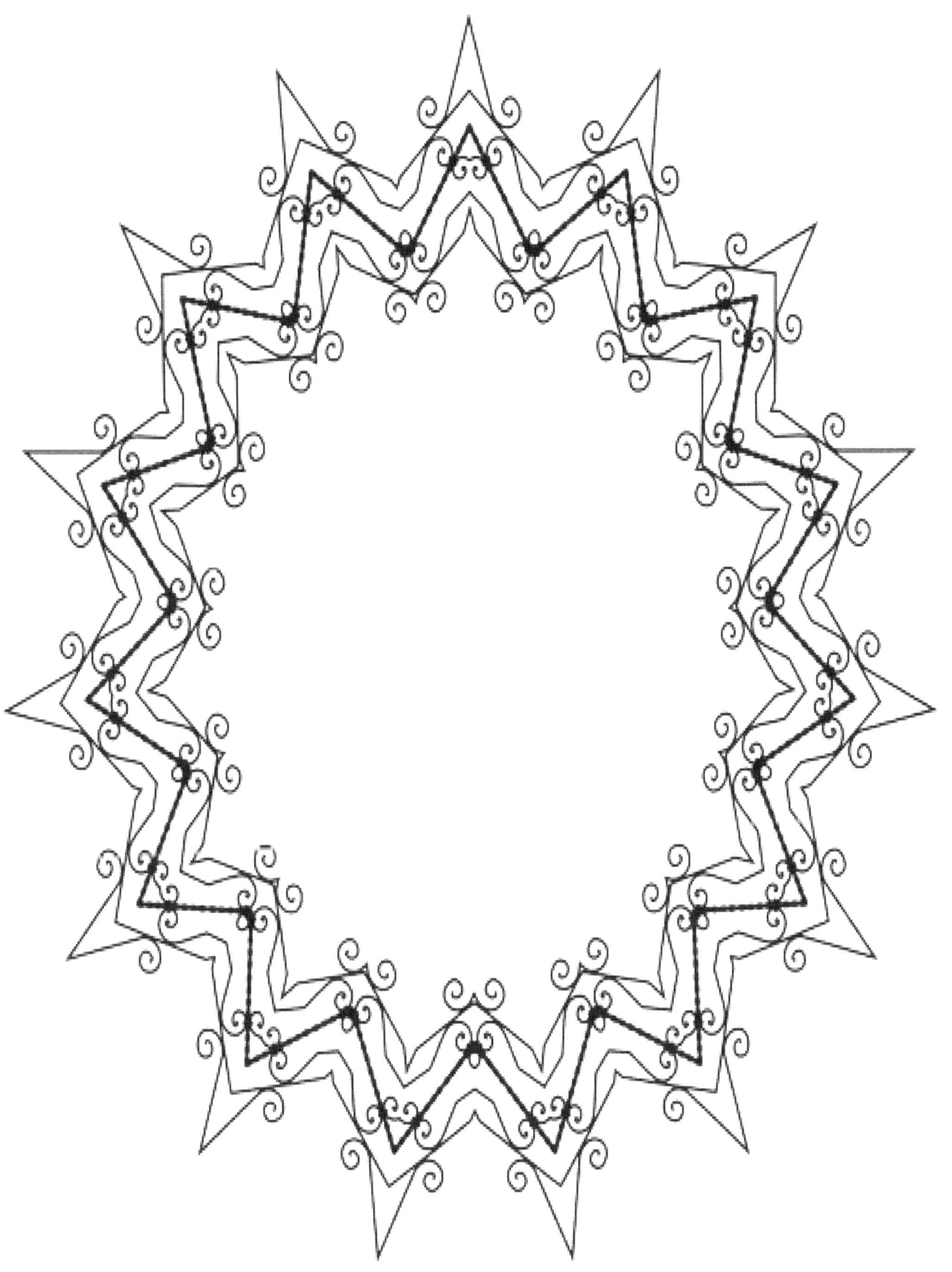

blank for bleed

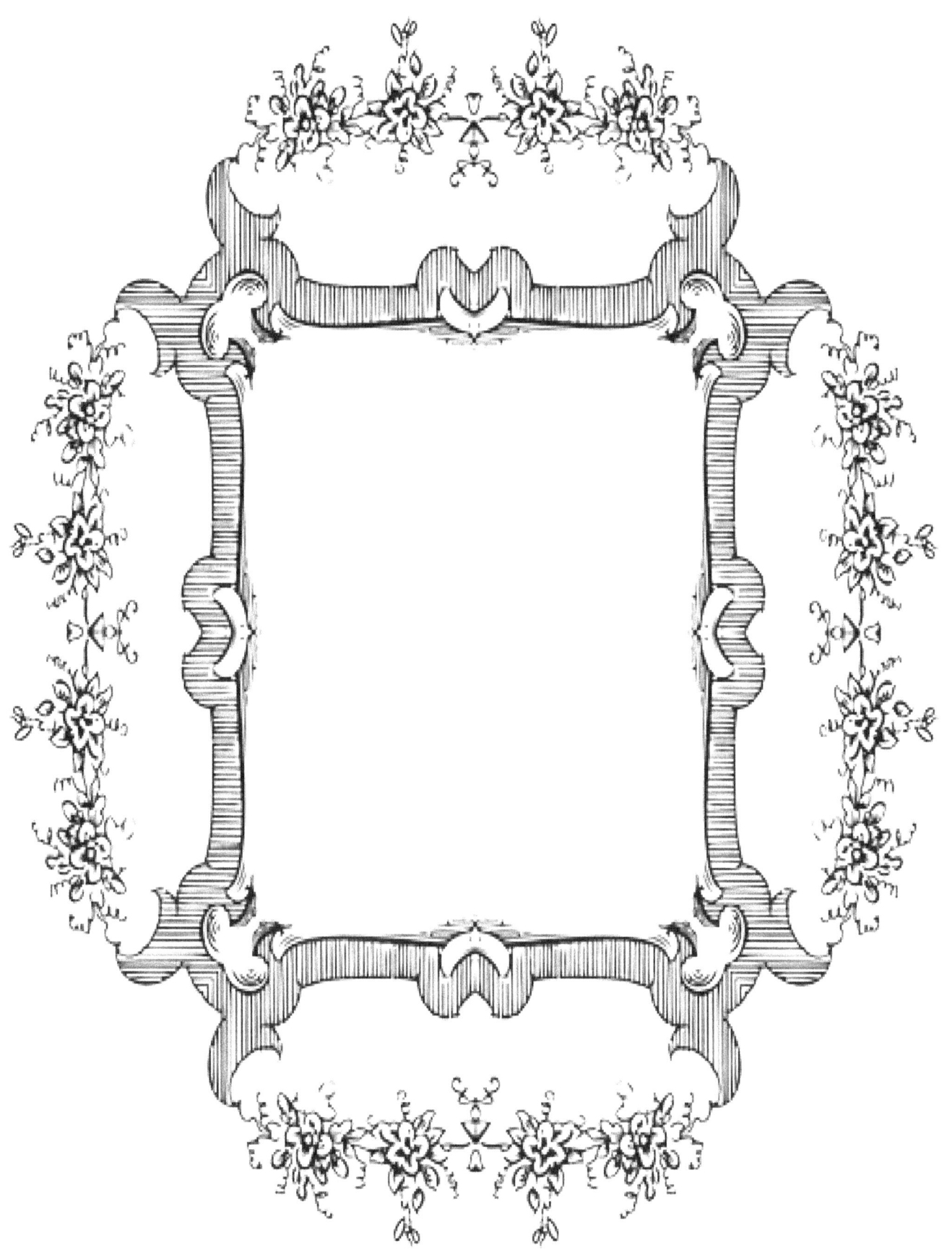

blank for bleed

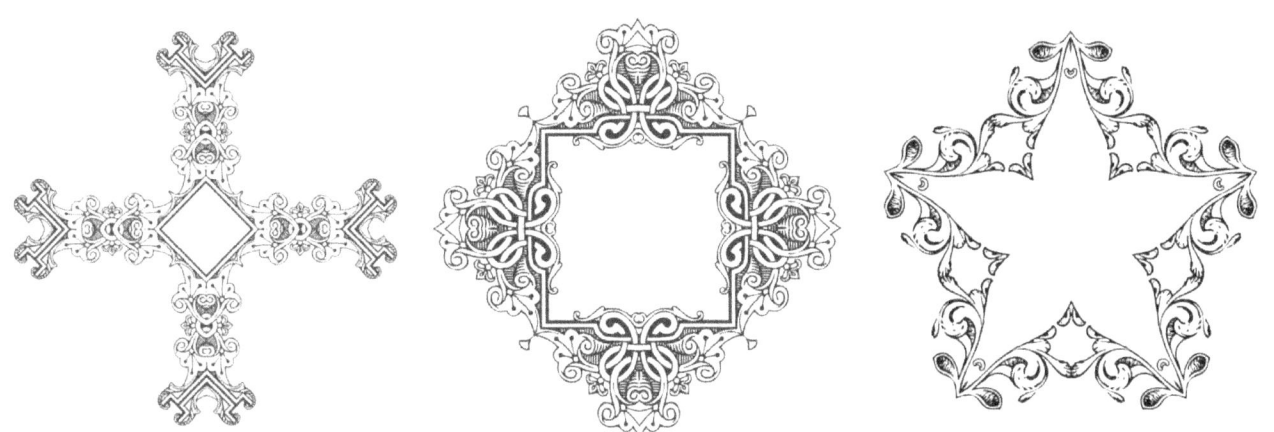

copyright@2020
Rhonda Ragan Shuck
All rights reserved. No part of this book may be reproduced, stored in a retrieval system, or transmitted in any form or by any means- electronic, mechanical, photocopy, recording, or any other-except for brief quotations in printed reviews, without the prior permission of the author.

All images are public domain and acquired at publicdomainvectors.org

www.ingramcontent.com/pod-product-compliance
Lightning Source LLC
Chambersburg PA
CBHW080505220526
45465CB00006B/2378